PROPHETS OF THE LORD

Also by Mary Evans
WOMAN IN THE BIBLE

PROPHETS

OF THE

LORD

Mary Evans

THE PATERNOSTER PRESS

British Library Cataloguing in Publication Data

Evans, Mary J.
Prophets of the Lord.
1. Bible. Prophets
I. Title
220.829163

ISBN 0-85364-483-7

Typeset by Photoprint, Torquay, Devon
and Printed in Great Britain for The Paternoster Press,
by The Guernsey Press Co. Ltd., Guernsey, Channel Islands.

*To Malcolm, June, Grace,
Gordon and Maureen*

CONTENTS

SECTION III – UP TO THE EXILE

SECTION IV – THE EXILE AND AFTER

Foreword

'In the past God spoke to our forefathers through the
prophets at many times and in various ways, but in these
last days he has spoken to us through his Son' (Hebrews
1:1, 2).

The letter to Hebrew Christians goes on to tell us just
how great and glorious Christ and his work are. Does this
then mean that the Old Testament prophets are now out-
dated and obsolete? In practice if not in theory, many
Christians seem to assume this to be true. Apart from a
few key verses in chapters like Isaiah 6, 40; Jeremiah 31;
Ezekiel 34, 37; and a vague impression of the contents of
Hosea, Amos and Jonah, many of us have little idea of
what the prophets are all about and are not too sure of
their relevance. But the author of Hebrews would have
been horrified at such ignorance! His aim was to emphasize
the supremacy of Christ, not to suggest that the prophets
need no longer be read. On the contrary, he himself often
refers to the prophets and shows how their words deepen
our understanding of the person and work of Christ. The
New Testament makes it very clear that a knowledge and
understanding of the Old Testament scriptures, including
the prophets, is vitally important, although they must be
read in the light shed on them by Jesus Christ.

It would be tragic, however, if the prophetic books were
read only as a duty and not for their own sake. It is true
that some sections are very difficult for modern readers to

understand — some were probably difficult for the first readers as well! But the books as a whole are worth reading for many reasons. They are messages given by real people to real people in real situations. Sometimes those people are not so very different from ourselves and their experiences reflect our own. But even when the differences are great, we can learn a lot from the way God dealt with and through the prophets. It is fascinating and encouraging to see how God worked amongst both individuals and groups, sometimes rebuking, sometimes comforting, but always starting from where they were and pointing them towards where he wanted them to be. The prophets' teaching about what God is like is assumed and built on in the New Testament, but much of it is not repeated. If therefore we want to know all that we can know of God, then we must read the prophets. Teaching about what God expects from his own people may need to be interpreted in the context of a different culture and social system, but we are left in no doubt about God's standards.

The aim of this book is to give you, the reader, an outline awareness of the content and meaning of the prophetic books. The purpose is not to make it unnecessary to read the prophets themselves. In fact my aim is that having read here about the prophets you won't be able to help yourself from going back to the Scriptures and re-reading the books there. Even if I have failed to make them irresistible, go and re-read the prophets anyway! Doing so may occasionally be difficult, but it may also be challenging, comforting, frightening, unsettling, inspiring, stimulating and even, at times, fun — it will certainly be worthwhile.

This book deals with the classical three larger ('major') and twelve shorter ('minor') prophetic books. In the Hebrew Old Testament the book of Daniel is placed alongside Psalms, Proverbs, etc. among the 'Writings' rather than with the prophets. Daniel himself is portrayed as a statesman who interpreted dreams and had visions, rather than a prophet as such. Therefore, and because space is not unlimited, the book of Daniel, important as it is, must be left for another occasion. The prophetic books have been arranged in largely chronological order, although for convenience the three books whose date is most disputed, Obadiah, Jonah and Joel are placed at the end of Section III.

It is appropriate at this point to add a note of thanks to my friends, students and colleagues for their support and stimulation, to Edna Sansom for her help in preparing the script, and in particular to Peter Cousins of Paternoster Press, who, through his help and advice given during the editing process, has made an invaluable contribution to the book in its final form.

NOTE ON THE QUESTIONS FOR STUDY AND DISCUSSION

Some questions are aimed at those who are entering for academic examinations and are therefore primarily concerned with an objective analysis of the material. Others are directed to those whose primary concern is the teaching of the prophets and its application in their own lives. Many questions will in fact be relevant to both these groups, but readers should note this distinction and be selective in their use of the study and discussion material.

SECTION I

Introduction

CHAPTER 1

Who Were the Prophets?

In the Old Testament a prophet is somebody who is called by God to perform a task or a set of tasks for him, and in particular to deliver a message from him. God called people with very different personalities in very different situations to do and say different things. So it is not surprising that we find a great deal of variety amongst the prophets and we must beware of making our definition too narrow. Occasionally, the term prophet is used simply to refer to pious people who are obviously in close relationship with God; the reference to Abraham in Genesis 20:7 seems to come into this category. More often, prophets are referred to as 'men of God' (1 Kings 13). It is possible that there was at some stage a distinction between a prophet (*nabi*) and a seer (*ro'eh*) but later on the two terms are used synonymously (1 Samuel 9:9).

However, though it was 'at many times and in various ways' that God spoke 'through the prophets' (Hebrews 1:1), it was the same God who spoke in each case and, as we shall see, there is also a great deal of consistency in the ministry and messages of the prophets. The first responsibility of any prophet was to ensure that he himself (or herself; there are several women described as prophets) was in a right relationship with God — for it would be impossible for anyone not themselves right with God to fulfil their mission. Their responsibilities were different, but they were all called both by their example and by their

teaching to help Israel, as a nation called to be the people
of God, to live in right relationship with him.

VARIETY AND UNITY

The Old Testament shows great variety in the way prophets
worked. Some worked as individuals, completely independent of other prophets or prophetic groups and also
of the official organization of the state religion. In fact
Elijah at one time felt so isolated that he came to believe
there was nobody else in the whole of Israel who was still
seeking to obey God (1 Kings 19:10, 14)! Other prophets
seem to have gathered together in semi-official groups.
Elisha, though often himself working independently, had
strong connections with these groups (2 Kings 2:3–5; 4:38;
9:1; cf 1 Samuel 10:5; 19:20). Sometimes music was used
by prophets to assist in their work (Exodus 15:20–21; 1
Samuel 10:5; 2 Kings 3:15). Sometimes prophets spoke in
very clear and down to earth terms, on other occasions
they used dreams or ecstatic speech, though Jeremiah
makes it clear that every prophet is responsible for his
own words and the claim that 'I had a dream' carries no
guarantee that the prophet's message is from God (Jeremiah
23).
   Some of the prophets and the groups of prophets
appear to have been particularly associated with certain
religious shrines, as Samuel was with Shiloh, at least for
a time (1 Samuel 3:19–21). Prophets like Nathan in the
reign of David (2 Samuel 7:1–7; 12:1–15; 1 Kings 1), or
Isaiah in the reign of Hezekiah (2 Kings 19:1–7,20–37; 20:4–
11; Isaiah 36–39), were well-known national statesmen
and trusted royal advisors. On the other hand there were
prophets like Amos who appear to have concentrated on
speaking to the ordinary Israelite rather than being involved
in national politics and others like Elijah (1 Kings 18:16–17),
Micaiah (1 Kings 22:8), or Jeremiah (Jeremiah 26:1–24;
36:1–32), who at times were treated by the king as enemies
of the state.

For some, whether they worked individually or in groups, prophecy was a full time career, whereas others were unexpectedly called by God from quite different situations. Amos explains that although his background was in farming not in prophecy, nevertheless God had called him to bring a clear prophetic message to Israel and he was not going to be diverted from his task simply because a professional prophet from the local shrine objected to what he was saying (Amos 7:14–15). A number of prophets worked for a long period of time, sometimes stretching over the reigns of several kings (Hosea 1:1; Micah 1:1). But some, like Saul and his men, seem to have been given a prophetic gift on one particular occasion (1 Samuel 19:20–24). Sometimes people who wanted to discover God's will in a specific situation went to find the prophets to ask their advice (1 Kings 22:6–28; 2 Kings 22:13–20). On other occasions the prophet deliberately sought people out in order to deliver God's message to them (2 Samuel 12:1; 1 Kings 19:15–17).

The prophets certainly were a mixed bunch, and we can begin to see something of what the author of Hebrews meant when he described God as speaking through the prophets in many different ways (1:1). But this tremendous variety does not mean that the prophets were simply isolated individualists speaking of their own accord and with no real connection between them. In fact the prophets were very conscious that they were part of a long and consistent tradition. They often quote earlier or even contemporary prophets (Jeremiah 26:18–19; Isaiah 2:1–4; Micah 4:1–4). They see themselves as recalling Israel to the truth which the nation should already have known and understood; as bringing not a new message but rather a new awareness of the reality of God's involvement in everyday life and of the importance of their relationship with him (Micah 6:8). Nor should we see a prophet's work as consisting only of bringing messages from God, whether proclamations of judgment or of hope, or lessons about what God was like and what were his particular requirements of Israel at that time. They were also responsible to pray for the people, and by the way they lived out their own lives to show what it meant to be in relationship with God.

Certainly, the message of each prophet applied to a specific situation and was given to a specific group of people, but it is very clear that the recognized prophets were all relating to and speaking of and from one and the same God, Yahweh, the sovereign Lord. The emphasis may at times be different, but they all knew and presented God as the one who is opposed to injustice and hypocrisy and who seeks righteousness and faithfulness. He loves Israel deeply and longs for them to relate to him, but he cannot and will not tolerate half-hearted service or worship shared with another. The prophets agree that God is the Lord of history; that is, he is present and active not in some separate mystical realm but in real everyday events. But he is also the one who is in control of the universe and therefore his word can be depended upon absolutely.

FALSE PROPHETS

Deuteronomy 18:15–22 is an important passage for our understanding of prophecy in Israel. Verses 15, 16 relate the work of the prophets to that of Moses in terms of their responsibility to convey God's words to the people and the people's responsibility to heed what the prophets are saying. In addition v18 has rightly been seen as messianic, as looking forward to the coming of the one great prophet who would be able to speak God's words with complete confidence and conviction and with no possibility of mistake. But as verses 20–22 make clear, the promise relates also to those who in the meantime take up the prophetic role. This chapter emphasizes the fact that not everyone who claimed to speak on God's behalf is recognized in the Old Testament as a legitimate prophet. There were people who, whether out of self-interest or greed, or because they wanted to encourage or please their hearers, or for any other reason, gave messages which in no sense could be seen as conveying the will or the word of God. Jeremiah 23:9–40 and Micah 2:6–11 also describe the actions of such 'prophets' and the attitude of God towards them.

Elsewhere in Deuteronomy 18, and in other parts of the Old Testament, prophecy is clearly distinguished from a whole range of practices which are seen as detestable and strictly forbidden in Israel. 'Let no one be found among you who sacrifices his son or daughter in the fire, who practises divination or sorcery, interprets omens, engages in witchcraft, or casts spells, or who is a medium or a spiritist or who consults the dead. Anyone who does these things is detestable to the Lord' (Deuteronomy 18:10–12). What we have here is a strict rule against trying to predict the future by any other method than listening to what God has to say to his people. Anyone using these occult methods and anyone who speaks in the name of any other god (Deuteronomy 18:20) is not and must never be seen as a prophet of Yahweh, the Lord God of Israel, no matter what their message might be. In fact Israel's law required that such people be executed.

But assuming that a prophet was not using this kind of practice: how then could anyone know whether his message was from God or not?

If a prophetic message involved prediction, then the solution appears fairly straightforward. 'If what a prophet proclaims in the name of the LORD does not take place or come true, that is a message the LORD has not spoken' (Deuteronomy 18:22). Similarly, 'The prophet who prophesies peace will be recognized as one truly sent by the LORD only if his prediction comes true' (Jeremiah 28:9. Note that most versions of the bible use 'LORD' in capitals, as a translation for Yahweh, the Old Testament personal covenant name for God).

The question of fulfilment is sometimes rather less straightforward, because it is clear that many prophecies have what might be called a built-in 'if'. Thus when Jonah predicted the total destruction of Nineveh, although he does not say *'If you do not repent'*, this condition is understood quite clearly to be included. Thus the fact that the destruction did not happen as he had said it would, did not automatically mean that Jonah was a false prophet. The conditional nature of many prophecies, where their fulfilment or non-fulfilment depends on the action or reaction of the hearers, explains why some clearly recognized prophets were not rebuked for making prophecies which apparently were never fulfilled.

The fact that prophecy is often conditional makes it difficult at times to assess accuracy of prediction but such accuracy still remains an essential prerequisite for a prophet to be recognized as genuine. However, the fact that a prophet can accurately predict certain events is not sufficient to guarantee his prophetic credentials. The message of a prophet may be accompanied by all kinds of miraculous happenings but if what is said does not tie in with what God has already revealed about himself, then it is not to be heeded. 'If a prophet, or one who foretells by dreams, appears among you and announces to you a miraculous sign or wonder, and if that sign or wonder of which he has spoken takes place, and he says, "Let us follow other gods . . . and worship them", you must not listen to the words of that prophet or dreamer' (Deuteronomy 13:2–3). The message of a true prophet will always be in accord with what God has previously revealed in other ways.

Jeremiah 23:9–40 makes clear in no uncertain terms another essential characteristic of a prophet of Yahweh. He will live a holy life. 'Among the prophets of Jerusalem I have seen something horrible. They commit adultery and live a lie. They strengthen the hands of evildoers, so that no-one turns from his wickedness' (v14). A true prophet is one whose message does not contradict known teaching and whose life reflects the message he brings showing that he really is in relationship with the holy, righteous, loving God.

CHAPTER 2

Prophetic Literature

The primary job of all the prophets was to speak out God's word to the people to whom God sent them. Clearly, much of the material recorded in the prophetic books is simply *written reports of what were originally spoken messages*. Amos, probably the first of the written prophetic works to be compiled, consists almost totally of this kind of material. But the prophetic books, particularly the later ones, also contain *narrative descriptions* of events that occurred in the lives of the prophets; sometimes personal accounts in the first person and sometimes third person descriptions. We also find records of *the prophet's own prayers and praises*, or of their own *personal spiritual struggles* and sometimes included are *messages which were in written form from the beginning* (Jeremiah 36).

It will be helpful to consider some of the types of material included in the prophetic writings, so that we may be better equipped, to recognize different categories. Then, as we read through the prophetic books, we shall be able to understand the various sections within their own context.

LOOKING TO THE FUTURE

One of the major tasks of the prophet seems to have been to open up the future to the people of Israel. This does

not mean that they offered a clear blue-print of some
future programme of events; their purpose was to demonstrate how God was at work in the world and to show the
consequences of Israel's actions. All the prophetic announcements of the future are really about God acting in
the world either in salvation or in judgment. They are
almost always found in the context of condemnation of
present behaviour, or a challenge to repent and take up
new patterns of behaviour.

Accusations against Israel

Almost all the prophetic books include sections explaining
the reasons why God is going to judge his people.
Throughout most of her history, Israel saw herself as 'all
right really'; they were the people of God, fulfilling the
necessary religious duties commanded in the law, bringing
the right sacrifices, and so on. The prophets realized that
this was not the way that God saw things, and spelled out
in some detail the ways in which Israel fell short of God's
requirements. It was important that the people of Israel
should have a correct view of themselves, and should
recognize that they were sinners who had not kept their
part of the covenant that God had made with them.

Keeping the covenant was not just a matter of fulfilling
outward obligations, of attending the proper feasts and
bringing the proper sacrifices. Being in covenant relationship with a holy, loving and merciful God brought with it
a responsibility that they too should be holy, loving and
merciful, so that people from other nations would know
something of what God was like by looking at the way in
which Israel behaved. The prophets condemn Israel, not
simply in general abstract terms, but for very down-to-
earth specific sins, mostly in the areas of oppression,
injustice, immorality and idolatry. All these things were
denials of God and his character (Amos 2:6–16; 5:11–13;
6:1–7; Hosea 12; Ezekiel 11:1–12; 14:1–11 etc.).

Sometimes these accusations against Israel are actually

presented in the form of a legal case, God bringing an action against his people for failing to keep the covenant. Here the account includes an introductory call for a hearing; questioning of witnesses (sometimes the earth itself is called to act as a witness!); an address by the prosecution usually showing what God had done for Israel and how little reason they had to turn against him; a statement explaining that it was useless to try and put things right simply by using the sacrificial system; a declaration of guilt; and a pronouncement of the sentence of destruction. Micah 6 is a good example of this kind of account, and similar covenant lawsuits are found in Isaiah 1; 42:18–25; 50:1–3; and Jeremiah 2.

Prophecies of Disaster

The terminology used in these prophecies is varied. One might speak of punishment, another of judgment, of destruction or doom or ruin, but the point is the same. Prophet after prophet announces that because of the behaviour of those addressed, God will punish them and some kind of disaster will come upon them. Sometimes the prophecy is directed against particular individuals or groups (2 Kings 1:2–4; Amos 7:16–17; Jeremiah 28:15–17), sometimes against the whole nation of Israel (Amos 4:1–2; Hosea 2:5–7; Micah 3:1–4, 9–12; Isaiah 8:6–8; 30:12–14; Jeremiah 5:10–14; 7:16–18, 20), sometimes even against the enemies of Israel (Amos 1 and 2; Isaiah 7, 8 and 10). In each case, the pattern of the written account is very similar.

First comes a statement to attract the attention of the reader: 'Hear the word of the Lord', 'Hear this word', 'Listen', or some similar phrase. This is followed by the accusation, sometimes stated briefly and then explained more fully, and the announcement of what the punishment will be, often preceded by the statement, 'This is what the Lord says'.

Calls to Repent

However clearly and strongly they prophesied doom and disaster, the prophets were very clear that this need not be the end of the story. They constantly taught that the better way would be for their hearers to repent and to change their life-style so that they could be restored to a full relationship with God. Not only do the prophets constantly plead with Israel — they portray God as also pleading with Israel to repent so that he can forgive them and pour blessings upon them. These calls to repentance are sometimes regarded as part of the prophecies of disaster and sometimes as part of the announcements of salvation but they are worth looking out for as recognizable elements of the prophets' message in their own right.

They usually involve a call to return, to seek the Lord, to break with the past and to begin afresh (Amos 5:4–5; Jeremiah 3:12–13; 4:1–2; Zephaniah 2:1–3). These prophecies are often found at a pivotal point, after a prophet has spoken of disaster and destruction and before he goes on to speak of hope for the future beyond the turning point of repentance. This demonstrates an underlying understanding that prophecies both of punishment and of salvation are frequently conditional, even when, as in the case of Jonah prophesying the destruction of Nineveh, that condition is not specifically mentioned.

Announcements of Salvation

Pronouncements of the way in which God will intervene on behalf of his people, whether individuals or the nation as a whole, to rescue them from particular situations of difficulty and defeat are also typical of the prophets. Such pronouncements are sometimes given in response to a request for help, a lament or petition brought in a specific situation, and they are used to express God's reassurance to Israel. Often the promised salvation refers to a very definite situation in the present, but sometimes it is directed to future situations which have not yet developed, or even to the last days, God's final intervention in history.

The pattern of these pronouncements is very similar to the pattern of predictions of disaster. Not all these elements occur every time, but in general there is a call to attention; a description of the situation and the need involved; a promise that God will intervene on behalf of those in need; a description of the results of God's action; and a statement of God's purpose in taking the action he does. God's purpose often involves more than simply making sure that his people are blessed, he is concerned that the whole world should recognize his power and his glory. (Isaiah 41:8–13,17–20; 42:14–17; 44:1–5; 49:7–12; Jeremiah 33:14–15; 35:18–19; Ezekiel 37:21–28). Note that the pattern is the same whether the prophecy is true or false (Jeremiah 28:2–4)!

TEACHING TECHNIQUES

All sorts of means and methods are used by the prophets to get across the teaching that is essential if the people are really to understand what God is like and where they stand in relation to him. Some of these methods simply reflect the varied ways in which God spoke to the prophets themselves, but others are apparently related to the personal gifts and skills of the individual concerned.

Visions

One way in which God communicated with the prophets was through visions of various kinds, and reports of these visions are common in the prophetic literature. Typically, these reports begin with an opening formula, such as 'I saw', or 'God showed me', often accompanied by a historical note explaining what was going on at the time when the vision occurred, as 'In the year that King Uzziah

died' (Isaiah 6:1). This is followed by a description of what
the prophet saw or what happened to him in the vision.
Finally, in cases where the meaning is not self-evident,
there may be an explanation of the purpose and significance
of the vision, of what God intended the prophet and the
people to learn from it.

Because these reports are autobiographical, that is, they
describe an experience which the prophet himself has
actually gone through, the message they contain comes
across with particular force and urgency. But, significantly,
the emphasis is almost always not on the prophet and
what he has seen and undergone, but on the lessons he
has learned and wishes to pass on to his hearers. Visions
vary in length; Amos 7:1–8 contains a description of three
separate visions — locusts stripping the land, fire destroying the land and a plumb-line measuring the land —
whereas the whole of Ezekiel 8:1 to 11:25 is an extended
report of a single vision. Other examples of visionary
experiences are found in Isaiah 6:1–13; Jeremiah 24:1–10;
Ezekiel 37:1–14; 40:1 – 48:35; Amos 8:1–6.

Symbolic Actions

In several of the prophetic books we find accounts of
actions performed by the prophet or on his behalf. These
actions are symbolic of the way in which God intends to
act towards his people. There is a link between this kind
of account and the visions, because it was sometimes in a
vision that the prophet received his instructions to perform
a particular act. As might be expected, the accounts contain
God's instruction to perform the action, a description of
the action itself, and an explanation of its meaning. They
sometimes also include a statement made to onlookers.

The prophet may be instructed to make something, as
when Ezekiel was told to build a model of Jerusalem under
siege (Ezekiel 4:1–3); or to do something, as when Jeremiah
buried a linen belt or broke a pot (Jeremiah 13:1–11; 19:

1–13); or to act in a particular way, as when Ezekiel was told not to mourn openly when his loved wife died (Ezekiel 24:15–24). As with the vision reports, the emphasis in the text is not on the action but on the lesson conveyed by the action, usually that God was going to act either against, or on behalf of his people (Isaiah 8:1–4; Ezekiel 4:4 to 5:17; 37:15–28; Hosea 1:2–11).

Parables and Illustrations

As well as visions and symbolic actions the prophets often used parables, allegories, well-known proverbs or sayings, or everyday object lessons to get their point across. In Isaiah 5:1–7, Israel is compared to a vineyard where, in spite of all the efforts of its owner, all that will grow are useless wild grapes. Jeremiah pictures Israel as clay in the potter's hands (18:1–12), and Ezekiel, in a series of pictures, sees them as, amongst other things, the wood from a vine which is only fit for burning, a deprived and abandoned baby, and a prostitute (Ezekiel 15 to 17). See also Jeremiah 16:14–18; 31:29–30; Ezekiel 18:1–4; Haggai 1:3–11.

Laments and Hymns

Some of the prophets are more expert in and make more use of poetry than others, but the use of laments and hymns of thanksgiving and praise to describe God's attitude to Israel and what should be Israel's attitude to God is also common. The laments may be prompted by personal trouble, or the fate of Israel, or that of nations opposed to Israel. They may be expressed as the words of the prophet, of the nation or even of God himself. (Isaiah 10:1–11; 18:1–6; Jeremiah 9:16–21; Ezekiel 19:1–14; 32:1–16; Amos 5:1–3; Micah 7:1–6). Praises and hymns of thanksgiving may refer to some specific act of God or may simply celebrate his person, works and character (Isaiah 12:1–6;

25:1 to 26:21; 42:10–17; 63:7–19; Jeremiah 31:3–14; Micah 7:14–20).

PERSONAL EXPERIENCES

Several of the shorter prophetic books seem to be directed simply to getting across one particular point and in these we may learn very little about the prophet himself. However, especially in the longer books or where the teaching covers broader ground, the life and experiences and understanding of the individual prophet becomes part of the message.

Call narratives

One of the most significant areas in a prophet's experience was his conviction of being called by God to the task that he had undertaken. Whether they came from a priestly background, or from within one of the prophetic groups, or were simply brought out of an ordinary occupation, it seems that most of the prophets had had a particular encounter with God when he had called them to this work. Often the form of that call influenced the course of their ministry, as Isaiah's overwhelming experience of God's glory and God's holiness is constantly reflected in his writings. The experience itself was a personal one which had a profound effect on the prophet, but recording the event, in what appears to be a somewhat stylized form, apparently acted as a kind of public accreditation. The fact of a prophet's call to speak on God's behalf supported his right to do so.

It is perhaps significant that the pattern of call narratives appears to be related to the call of Moses: in addition to the actual commissioning by God, we often find the prophet questioning his own ability to do the job, and an account of God's further reassurance, sometimes supported by a sign. (Isaiah 6:1–13; Jeremiah 1:4–19; Ezekiel 1:1 to 3:15. See also 1 Kings 22:19–20 and Amos 7:14–16).

Personal Struggles

There are a number of accounts in the first person where the prophets describe their own work. These narratives are helpful in giving us historical perspective; they are often parallel to descriptions of the same events in the historical books. For example, Isaiah 36:1 to 39:8 is repeated in 2 Kings 18:13 to 20:21, and Jeremiah 39 and 52 cover the same ground as 2 Kings 25. However as well as the factual accounts of the prophets' work, we are often given information about their personal struggles, both external and internal.

Almost all of the prophets suffered because of apathy and indifference to their message or even direct opposition whether this was experienced in the form of mockery from the people to whom they spoke or ill-treatment and persecution from national leaders (Isaiah 28:9–22, Jeremiah 37 to 38, Ezekiel 2:4–5; 33:30–33; Hosea 9:11; Micah 2:6; etc.). Often they were driven to speak out and contradict other prophets and cultic officials who also claimed to be speaking in God's name; we are made aware of the tension that this caused in the prophet (Jeremiah 23:17–22; 28:1–17; Micah 3:5,11). In this connection, we may note that the prophets are not portrayed as spiritual giants who never had any personal doubts. Jeremiah in particular lets us see something of his own doubt and personal torment concerning what God was doing in Israel (Jeremiah 11: 18–23; 20:7–10).

Prayers

One of the ways in which we get a picture of how the prophets felt and reacted is in the accounts of their prayers. Here we can see something of their hopes and fears for Israel but also the development of their own relationship with God, and their personal experience of joy and sorrow. Some of these prayers are brief and express an immediate reaction to feelings or to circumstances. Others are longer and give a more thought out response. Sometimes God's reply to the prayer is recorded, on other occasions it is left to the reader to recognize God's answer for themselves (Isaiah 6:8,11; Jeremiah 12:1–13; 20:7–18, 32:17–44; Jonah 2:2–10; 4:1–4; Habakkuk 3:1–19).

These prayers, along with the records of the prophets' personal pilgrimages, help us to see the prophets as real people, with real feelings and real problems doing a job in an actual situation; rather than as abstract thinkers presenting philosophical or even theological truths but with no real identity of their own.

CHAPTER 3

Historical Overview

If we are to understand fully the message of the prophets we need to know something not only of their own immediate background situation but of the whole history of Israel. All the prophets are conscious of Israel's history and of the way in which God has worked in Israel in the past. Often it is their awareness of the past that enables them to identify God's purposes in the present and to look forward to God's action in the future. This means that we too need to have some knowledge of what has gone before and of where each particular prophet fits into the whole picture. For this purpose we are not concerned with modern questions about the meaning of history, or even questions about the accuracy of the accounts, but with the history of Israel as it was understood by the prophets, a story of obedience and disobedience, judgment and mercy.

It is possible to gain an historical perspective by reading straight through parts of the Pentateuch and the books of Samuel and Kings, but it is not always easy to see exactly what is going on there unless we already have some knowledge of the whole situation. So before looking at the historical background to individual prophets, we shall attempt an overview of the whole scene.

FROM ABRAHAM TO SAMUEL

Most of the prophets that we shall be considering were

active during the monarchy, the period when Israel was governed by a king. But Israel's history and thus the context in which the prophets saw themselves, commenced much earlier. It could be said that Israel began with Abraham, when God made a covenant, a kind of treaty or contract, with him, promising that through his son Isaac, Abraham would have many, many descendants who would possess a land of their own to inhabit. However, it is perhaps more realistic to see the start of Israel as a nation as occurring several hundred years later. It was probably about 1280 BC, when Moses led the Israelites (named after Abraham's grandson who, with his whole family, had emigrated to Egypt in a time of famine) in the Exodus from Egypt.

When the Israelites were camped at Mount Sinai, not long after leaving Egypt, God made another covenant, this time with the whole nation (Exodus 19,24). In this solemn agreement, God, who had revealed himself to Moses as Yahweh, the One who IS, the One who is real and present and will reveal himself in his actions (Exodus 3:14–15), now committed himself to Israel. He promised to be their God, looking after their interests and uniting them in a personal relationship with himself. As part of this covenant the people of Israel were responsible for giving God their wholehearted loyalty and for living in a way which reflected their status as his people. This meant that they were bound to keep the laws which had been given to Moses on the mountain.

From this point on, the history of Israel is presented as the story of how the nation, repeatedly broke their side of the covenant with God. Time and time again they were given another chance as God chose to remain faithful to them, although the covenant would technically be invalidated when one side broke it. The history showed how God used all kinds of means to try and bring them to a sense of responsibility and repentance for their actions, and to bring them back into a right relationship with himself. Sometimes he gave them great prosperity to make them aware of his goodness to them. When in those circumstances they still turned to other gods he brought disasters to them so that they would turn to him. Often he used faithful individuals, to assist or rebuke or remind or challenge their fellow countrymen.

In fact, they broke the covenant almost before it was properly ratified. They encouraged Aaron to make an image to represent the 'gods' who had brought them out of Egypt (Exodus 32). Shortly afterwards, when the time came to enter the land that Yahweh had promised to them, they showed that their commitment to him had been a very superficial one, preferring to return to Egypt rather than to trust that God really was able to keep his promise to them (Numbers 13, 14). It was this lack of trust that caused their entry to the promised land to be postponed while they wandered through the wilderness areas for forty years. During this time God used Moses to govern them and teach them the significance of the covenant.

Under Joshua's leadership, Israel eventually did take over the land of Canaan, but their renewed commitment to the covenant with Yahweh (Joshua 24) did not last. They continued to turn away from God, this time towards the gods of their new land. The book of Judges describes this period and although there are notable highlights, in general it tells a rather sad story of the nation constantly disobeying and rejecting God and getting themselves into all kinds of trouble. Even though Yahweh repeatedly sent men and women to lead them and deliver them, the people's response of trust and loyalty never lasted long. These leaders were known as 'judges', but their role seems to have been a mixture of military leader, prophet and sometimes priest as well.

The period of the judges ended when Israel became aware of two new needs. Protection against their enemies called for a continuous and consistent government embracing all twelve tribes. In addition a regular army was needed to withstand the Philistines in particular. Thus Samuel, the last and possibly the greatest of the judges, was asked to appoint a king for Israel so that there would be a continuing central focus for all the tribes. Samuel saw this as a denial of Yahweh as Lord and King of Israel and opposed it (1 Samuel 8). Nevertheless, at God's command he anointed Saul, the young man from the tribe of Benjamin, as Israel's first king.

THE EARLY MONARCHY AND THE DIVISION OF THE KINGDOM

Initially, Saul proved a first-rate leader and there was a growing sense of national unity. But soon he began to act as if being king gave him the right to make his own decisions without regard for God's commands. He was rejected as king (1 Samuel 15) and eventually replaced by David who, after a short period during which Saul's son Ishbosheth controlled the northern tribes, reigned over the whole of Israel. (2 Samuel 1–5).

David made Jerusalem his capital and during the thirty-three years of his reign there, Israel became used to government and worship being centralized. David brought the ark of the covenant to Jerusalem and organized plans for building a permanent temple there to replace the tent in which the ark had previously been kept (2 Samuel 6–7). At this time God made a further covenant, this time with David and his descendants. He promised that unlike that of Saul, the royal line founded by David would be permanent, although any individual descendant of David who turned against God would be disciplined, in later years the prophets realized that the people of Israel had come to think that the existence of the Davidic covenant reduced their own obligations. Believing that it was the king's responsibility to make sure that Israel was right with God, the people concluded they could safely ignore any responsibility placed upon them by the Sinai covenant.

Israel prospered under David and even more under his son Solomon. Surrounding nations were subdued or conquered and Israel's own boundaries extended. Everything seemed to be going well, but Solomon began to attach more importance to increasing his wealth and that of the nation than to keeping God's law. His son Rehoboam shared Solomon's arrogance but lacked his flair for government and for inspiring the loyalty of the people. In fulfilment of a previous prophecy of judgment (1 Kings 11), Israel rebelled against Rehoboam. Although he retained control of the southern region, known from that time on as the kingdom of Judah, the larger northern region became a separate kingdom whose first king was Jeroboam the son of Nebat. This division of the kingdoms took place round about 930 BC.

ISRAEL AND JUDAH EXIST TOGETHER

For the next two hundred years the two countries existed side by side, sometimes in an uneasy peace, sometimes at war with each other, and sometimes in alliance against more serious common enemies. A prophet had delivered to Jeroboam an offer of a covenant in virtually the same terms that had been given to David, that if he was faithful to God then his dynasty would be as enduring as David's (1 Kings 11:37–39). However, one of Jeroboam's first acts, as king of Israel, the northern kingdom, was to set up two golden calves as representations of God and to place them at shrines in Bethel and Dan. His intention was to dissuade Israelites from going into Judah to worship at the temple in Jerusalem, where they might be tempted to transfer their allegiance to the descendants of David.

Jeroboam's action established a pattern, and although occasionally complimentary things are said about a few of the nineteen different kings of Israel, every single one of them eventually receives a negative assessment in the account of their reign found in the books of Kings. Time after time we read the verdict that 'he did evil in the eyes of the Lord'. During the whole history of the northern kingdom, there were always a few people who remained faithful to Yahweh, a small number who responded to the warnings and teachings of the prophets. But the nation as a whole became decreasingly conscious of its identity as

the people of God. The covenant with Yahweh became
less and less important to them. Eventually divine judgment fell. There were to be no more chances for Israel.
The country was conquered by the Assyrians in 722 BC
and the people were taken into exile from which they
never returned. Only Judah was left to represent Yahweh
amongst the nations.

We know of four major prophets sent by God to try and
draw the northerners back into relationship with himself.
In the ninth century Elijah and Elisha were key figures in
the life of the nation. In the eighth century first Amos and
then Hosea challenged them about the spiritual poverty
which was afflicting the nation even at a time of apparent
national economic prosperity.

JUDAH ALONE

During the two hundred years that the two kingdoms
existed together Judah was consistently ruled over by
David's descendants (the only exception was a short
period when Queen Athaliah usurped the throne on the
death of her son Ahaziah, 2 Kings 11). Perhaps because
of this and because the temple in Jerusalem also served as
a reminder, Judah always showed a greater awareness of
the significance of the covenant and contained a higher
proportion of people who genuinely wanted to serve
God. However, even though about half of their kings
shared this commitment the nation as a whole moved
farther and farther away from God. As early as the eighth
century the prophets Isaiah and Micah warned that unless
there was a change of heart then Judah would come under
the same judgement as Israel and meet the same fate.

After Israel had been destroyed, a limited religious
reformation took place in Judah under Hezekiah (2 Kings
18–20). These reforms seem to have had little lasting effect
on the people's attitude and obedience to God. Certainly
in the first half of the seventh century, following the death
of Hezekiah there was a period of national moral and

religious corruption, led by the kings Manasseh and Amon (2 Kings 21), which was as bad as anything previously seen in either nation. This was followed by further reforms under Josiah, but in spite of Josiah's undoubted sincerity and his deep desire that the people should serve Yahweh, his reforms, like those of his great-grandfather Hezekiah had little lasting effect. Nahum, Zephaniah, Habakkuk, the prophetess Huldah and Jeremiah were all active during Josiah's reign.

The external threat from Assyria disappeared when in 612 BC Nineveh fell to the Babylonians, but Babylon now took Assyria's place as the major power in the area. Jeremiah indeed began to prophesy that Judah would be defeated by Babylon. This, he said, was God's judgment on Judah but it did not mean the end of Judah as a nation. After a period in exile God would bring them back into their own land. The prophecy was fulfilled when Judah came under Babylonian control after Babylon defeated Egypt in 605 BC. The Babylonians deported various groups to Babylon from about 597 BC, until after an unsuccessful attempt at rebellion, Jerusalem was besieged and finally destroyed in 587 BC.

THE EXILE AND THE RETURN TO THE PROMISED LAND

The major prophet amongst the exiles in Babylon was Ezekiel. Like Jeremiah, he insisted both that the exile was a judgment from God, and also that after the exile there was hope for those who repented and acknowledged Yahweh as Lord. The exile continued until Babylon fell to the Persians. Following this, the Persian emperor, Cyrus, issued a decree allowing the repatriation of all forced immigrants from other nations. The first group to return did so in 538 BC, led by Zerubbabel, but things did not move quite as quickly as many had hoped and it was not until about 516 BC, some seventy years after the fall of Jerusalem, that the temple was finally rebuilt.

The second half of the book of Isaiah refers to the return

from exile and the years afterwards. Zechariah and Haggai were both prophesying at this time. For various reasons it took many years to re-establish and rebuild the nation. The dates are not altogether certain, but it is probable that a further party returned from Babylon in 458 BC about eighty years after the first group. It was not until the last group came back with Nehemiah (perhaps around 445 BC), that the walls of Jerusalem were eventually rebuilt. The last of the writing prophets, Malachi, wrote his book round about this time.

CHAPTER 4

The Non-Writing Prophets

We know of several prophets who played an important part in the history of Israel but who left no written record of their teaching or work. The activities of these prophets may have been wider than the particular incidents recorded, but what is recorded concerning them helps to broaden our understanding of the prophetic ministry in general. We will consider the work of six such prophets.

NATHAN

On three important occasions in the life of David, the prophet Nathan plays a very significant role. First, at the institution of the Davidic covenant (2 Samuel 7; 1 Chronicles 17); then after David's adultery with Bathsheba (2 Samuel 12); and finally when the appointment of David's successor came into question. In spite of his undoubted importance we know very little about Nathan himself. He seems to have been a trusted advisor of David and a recognized prophet, but he appears on the scene without introduction and is not associated with any other event.

2 Samuel 7 shows David taking the initiative and asking Nathan's advice about his plan to build a permanent temple for the ark of God. In his role as a prophet Nathan assures David that his plans meet with God's approval. Later (verse 4), God speaks directly to Nathan saying that

he does not want David to build a temple. Yet God has a purpose for David and will bless him and his descendants in a unique way. This marks the institution of the Davidic covenant. Nathan's part in this indicates two important facts about the prophets. Firstly, that even a true prophet can come to a false conclusion if an idea seems good; and secondly, that a prophet should not be afraid to change his position and to explain the reason for doing so. There is no room for false pride when God speaks.

On the other two occasions it is Nathan himself who takes the initiative. With great tact and skill but also forcefully He warns David of how God views his behaviour towards Bathsheba and Uriah (2 Samuel 12:1–14). The adultery and murder are of course condemned but the strongest emphasis falls upon the meanness and selfishness of David's sin and upon his having acted as if his authority and status gave him the right to scorn God's word. Here, Nathan announces what is to become a constantly recurring theme in later prophets. The people of God, and, perhaps even more importantly, recognized leaders, must never behave in a way that will cause outsiders to think wrongly about God and his attitude towards sin and injustice (v. 14).

In 1 Kings 1 Nathan's action shows the political aspects of the prophet's role. He had intervened at Solomon's birth (2 Samuel 12:25) and now acts to make sure that in spite of Adonijah's machinations it is Solomon who succeeds David.

AHIJAH

Ahijah is less well known than Nathan, but his role in relation to Jeroboam I, the first king of the northern kingdom after the split with Judah, was very similar to Nathan's relationship with David. Ahijah was apparently a shrine prophet based at Shiloh (1 Kings 11:29). Even before Solomon's death he prophesied that because of Solomon's idolatry most of the kingdom would be taken from Solomon's descendants and given to Jeroboam. He relayed to Jeroboam God's promise of a covenant relationship exactly equivalent to the one he had made with David, involving an enduring dynasty (1 Kings 11:37–39). In response, Jeroboam waited for God to act, making no attempt to wrest the kingdom away from Solomon's son who thus had an opportunity to show he was different from his father.

However, having gained the northern throne, Jeroboam's trust in Yahweh seemed to leave him. As we have seen, he set up golden calf images as representations of Yahweh at shrines within Israel. When told that this was totally unacceptable to God, he did not respond to the rebuke in repentance as David had done, but insisted on going his own way (1 Kings 12:25 – 13:34). It was Ahijah's task therefore to tell Jeroboam that because he had rejected God and broken their relationship, his whole dynasty would be destroyed. The initial prophecy had depended for its fulfilment on Jeroboam's own response.

ELIJAH

Six chapters (1 Kings 17–19, 21; 2 Kings 1–2) concentrate on the life and ministry of Elijah and the stories about him are well known. He was an independent and apparently somewhat isolated prophet who came from Tishbe and who prophesied in the northern kingdom during the reigns of Ahab and Ahaziah (c874–850 BC). It is significant that the books of Kings, which were compiled in Judah long after the fall of the northern kingdom, nevertheless give such prominence to the two northern prophets Elijah and Elisha. It is suggested that two sources for the material about Elijah underlie these chapters. One seems to be a straightforward historical record of his prophetic activity as it affected the political religious and social life of Israel at that time; this was probably compiled not too long after Elijah's lifetime. The other is a compilation of personal anecdotes which reflect popular tradition and present Elijah as an almost legendary figure, emphasizing the miraculous element in the stories. There is certainly a distinction between the stories reflecting Elijah's national significance and those describing events in his personal life, but it is rather subjective to assume that miraculous events must necessarily be legendary.

Like the later prophets, who left more records of their teaching, Elijah's major concern appears to have been to bring the Israelites back to allegiance to Yahweh, an allegiance which appeared to him to have completely disappeared although there were actually still a significant number of committed Yahweh worshippers (1 Kings 18:3–4; 19:18). It was important that the Israelites should recognize that God was still active amongst them and that he would not tolerate their loyalty being transferred to Baal. The first we hear of Elijah is his prophecy of an extended drought, after which he not unnaturally disappeared from public view. The record of his being fed by ravens and cared for by a widow in Zarephath, and also of the healing of her son, are included to emphasize God's care for his servants.

The account in 1 Kings 18 of Elijah's dealings with Obadiah, with Ahab and with the prophets of Baal reads very realistically, and there is little reason to doubt the basic historicity of these events. (It has been suggested that Elijah's sacrifice was in fact ignited by lightning heralding the storm which would end the long drought.) The theological message here is clear; worshipping Baal was not simply incompatible with worshipping Yahweh, it was in itself a useless waste of time. Two misunderstandings which could arise from chapter 18 are quickly corrected in chapter 19. Firstly, although Elijah is a powerful man of God he is not superhuman but is as subject to fear, failure and depression as anyone else. Secondly, God does not speak only through dramatic 'mountaintop' experiences or spectacular phenomena, he also speaks quietly and intelligibly and in a way that takes the individual seriously.

Although Elijah's activities may have done much to encourage Yahweh worshippers and to prevent them being persecuted, they seem to have had little effect on

Ahab and his family. Personal judgment oracles are given to Ahab, after his treatment of Naboth (1 Kings 21), and to Ahaziah, when he attempted to discover the future through the Baal cult (2 Kings 1). Elijah was thus speaking out not simply against idolatry but also against social injustice and against seeking to discover the future by any other means than consulting Yahweh himself.

The account of Elijah's being taken up into heaven is as much a story of Elisha as it is of Elijah and in fact appears to be more in the pattern of the other Elisha narratives. The point of the narrative in its context is apparently to validate Elisha as a true successor of Elijah.

MICAIAH

We know of only one incident involving Micaiah, the son of Imlah (1 Kings 22), but it is apparent that he was known as a prophet and in particular as one who could be trusted not to shape his message to suit the king. Elijah was not the only believer in Yahweh active at the time, nor was he the only prophet with the courage to speak out against the establishment. The extent of Ahab's degeneracy is shown by the way he preferred to be deceived by comfort he suspected was false rather than face up to the truth. 1 Kings 22 provides a clear picture of the groups of official prophets which were available for consultation and of the way in which these prophets could easily be persuaded to pander to the vanity of rulers like Ahab. When later prophets like Micah condemned the official cultic prophets they were denouncing something which had been going on for a long time. It is interesting to note that Micah, perhaps in a deliberate attempt to identify himself with his earlier namesake, begins his prophecies by quoting Micaiah's final words (1 Kings 22:28; Micah 1:2).

ELISHA

Elisha, the son of Shaphat from Abel–Meholah, came from

a wealthy farming family (1 Kings 19:16,19–21). He was called to be a prophet soon after Elijah's encounter with God at Horeb and worked as such for about fifty years in Israel during the reigns of Ahab, Ahaziah, Jehoram, Jehu, Jehoahaz and Jehoash. Until Elijah departed from the scene Elisha acted as his personal servant (2 Kings 3:11) but on this occasion he asked for and was granted a 'double portion' of Elijah's spirit, symbolizing the inheritance of an eldest son who succeeds his father (2 Kings 2). He was certainly then recognized as successor to Elijah as a major prophet. He also apparently became leader of the prophetic communities working at the time.

There are fifteen separate incidents in Elisha's ministry as it is presented in 2 Kings 2:19 – 9:3; 13:14–20. In six of these he is portrayed as a national prophet giving advice and taking action in both the external and internal political affairs of the nation. He seems to have had little time for Jehoram, but out of respect for Jehoshaphat of Judah he gave vital advice in their joint campaign against Moab (2 Kings 3). He intervened against the Arameans (6:8–23), and prophesied in Samaria during an Aramean siege (6:24 – 7:20). He predicted the rise of two leaders who both subsequently rebelled against their predecessors, Hazael in Syria (8:7–15) and Jehu in Israel (9:1–13). By the time of his death he appears to have been accepted as a valuable national figure, and his final prophecy of further trouble with the Arameans was given when king Jehoash came for a 'death-bed' visit (13:14–20). Although the narrative describes the corruption of Ahab's descendants the aggressive fight against Baalism which so occupied Elijah's attention seems to have faded into the background.

There are three detailed descriptions of Elisha's dealings with a specific individual. Two of these relate to the Shunamite woman (4:8–37; 8:1–6) and the third to the healing of Naaman (5:1–27). Elisha's servant Gehazi is involved in all of these and it is possible that they came from a separate collection of stories. They are clearly intended to make various theological points about faith, about God's concern for those who serve him and about what is involved in being a servant of God.

The other six accounts are of brief undated incidents which seem to be included simply to enhance Elisha's reputation as a miracle worker (2:19–25; 4:1–7, 38–44; 6:1–7). At least four of these show how Elisha met the needs of prophetic communities and it has been suggested that they came from a compilation of stories about Elisha made within one of these communities and possibly influenced in their form by time and by hero-worship. It is from such stories that we learn much of what we know about the size and nature of the prophetic groups.

HULDAH

Almost all the prophets who are specifically mentioned in the historical books as being involved in national life after Elisha left written records of their teaching. It is perhaps significant that the major exception to this is Huldah. We are given an unusually detailed account of Huldah's background. She was 'the wife of Shallum son of Tikvah, the son of Harhas, keeper of the wardrobe. She lived in Jerusalem, in the Second District' (2 Kings 22:14). Jeremiah and Zephaniah were both active at the time, but when Josiah wanted to enquire of the Lord about the newly discovered 'book of the Law' it was from Huldah that his envoys sought an answer. She told them that Josiah was right to be worried about what the book revealed of the people's disobedience to God's law, but that God would respond to repentance and a commitment to serve him. Judah would eventually be punished, but not until after Josiah's reign. Thus, national disaster might be avoided, if only the whole nation would repent as Josiah himself had done.

There seems to have been no prejudice at this time against hearing God's word declared by a woman. Josiah's advisors, who were themselves all national leaders and included Hilkiah, the high priest, went to Huldah without apparent debate, to enquire about a matter of great spiritual and national significance, even though other sources of prophetic insight were available at the time. Similarly those who recorded the incident saw no need to comment on, let alone criticize, this procedure.

SECTION I: FURTHER STUDY

Questions for Study or Discussion

1. If there was so much variety amongst the prophets, can the term 'prophet' really be seen as having any consistent meaning?

2. In what circumstances, if any, could the Israelites be sure that any prophecy was 'true' or 'false'? Consider what these terms mean.

3. In what ways could a prophet's own experience become part of his ministry?

4. How can a knowledge of the different forms that the prophets used in their writing help us to understand a particular passage?

5. To what extent did the prophets receive messages directly from God and how far did their conclusions stem from their own thought and observation?

6. In what ways might ignorance of the historical circumstances in which a prophet wrote limit our understanding of his message?

7. Compare and contrast the ministries of Elijah and Elisha.

8. What aspects of the work and writings of the prophets should also be part of the work of the church today?

9. In a secular state is there any room for a Nathan or Ahijah to bring God's message to the ruling authorities?

10. How far do I allow my experiences to become part of my service of God?

SUGGESTED FURTHER READING

Blenkinsopp, J., *A History of Prophecy in Israel: from the settlement in the Land to the Hellenistic Period*, Westminster, 1983.

Bright, J., *A History of Israel*, SCM 1972.

Bullock, C.H., *An Introduction to the OT Prophetic Books*, Moody Press, 1986.

Koch, K., *The Prophets*, 2 vol. SCM 1983.

LaSor, W.S., (et al.), *Old Testament Survey*, Eerdmans, 1982.

von Rad, G., *The Message of the Prophets* SCM 1968.

Westermann, C., *Basic Forms of Prophetic Speech*, Lutterworth, 1967.

SECTION II

The Eighth Century Prophets

CHAPTER 5

Background to the Eighth Century Prophets

Amos and Hosea, who prophesied in Israel, together with
Isaiah and Micah who prophesied in Judah, are collectively
known as 'the eighth century prophets'. In fact all of them
prophesied and wrote in the second half of the eighth
century. Each has a distinctive perspective and an individual message, but the situations to which they spoke
were very similar and it is therefore useful to consider this
corporate background before looking at their individual
interests and concerns.

POLITICAL SITUATION

During the ninth century and particularly in its latter half,
Israel, the northern kingdom, had constantly been at odds
with the Arameans on her north-eastern border. (In some
versions of the Old Testament the Arameans are referred
to as Syrians; this is misleading, as the Aramean states are
not to be identified with modern Syria, although there is
some overlap in territory.) In spite of some recorded
successes, Israel often came off worst in their frequent
battles. At the end of the ninth century the power of the
Arameans was broken by Adad-nirari III of Assyria and
the Israelite army, which had been committed to repelling
the Aramean attacks, could be used in other directions.
From this time, Israel too, was compelled to pay a small

tribute to the increasingly influential Assyrians; but in general the Assyrians were still preoccupied elsewhere and Israel was left virtually alone. This state of affairs continued until the Assyrian ruler, Tiglath-Pileser III, came to power in 745 BC, and 'moved in' on Israel.

Egypt, the other major power in the area, was relatively weak during the first half of the eighth century. As a result there was a resurgence of Israelite power, and a period of prosperity which began under Jehoash (801–786 BC) and was consolidated during the long reign of Jeroboam II (786–746 BC). Jeroboam was an able ruler both politically and militarily and Israel's borders were both strengthened and extended.

Judah's history over this period is remarkably similar. There was a time of weakness in the latter part of the ninth century, caused by internal problems, inefficient governments and incursions by various foreign groups. This was followed by a time of increasing stability and prosperity, first under Amaziah (800–783 BC) and then under Uzziah (783–742 BC), whose forty year reign coincided almost exactly with that of Jeroboam II. The relationship between Israel and Judah during this period was reasonably settled and therefore both were able to expand, Israel in particular making inroads into territory previously held by the Arameans. This meant that by the middle of the eighth century the two nations between them controlled an area almost as great as that of Solomon's empire. So for more than fifty years there was a situation of political stability, expansionism, and national prosperity.

However, from 745 BC the power of Assyria became an increasingly significant factor, and the situation of the Hebrew kingdoms began to change. Israel vacillated between a policy of submission to Assyrian imposed taxes, and resistance, using Egypt as an ally. Assyria and Egypt had both regained strength and were vying for dominance in the area. In 733 Assyria acted forcefully to crush what it saw as Israel's rebellion and removed about half of Israel's territory from Israelite control. There was a brief respite until 724, when Israel's last king, Hoshea, led a revolt against Shalmaneser V and Assyria's response culminated in the siege and fall of Samaria which marked the end of Israel as a separate nation. Judah also came under heavy pressure at this time, but managed to survive in spite of some loss of territory and a number of serious crises including an unsuccessful siege of Jerusalem by Sennacherib's troops.

SOCIAL AND ECONOMIC CONDITIONS

During this period of growth and stability Israel and Judah controlled the important trade routes between Egypt and Assyria, an important source of revenue. The events of 748 BC give some indication of the nation's wealth. At this time, Menahem decided to strengthen his own position, as king of Israel, by supporting Assyria. For this purpose, he paid a tribute of 1000 talents collected from all the wealthy men each of whom paid 50 silver pieces (2 Kings 15:19–20). As a talent was approximately 30kg and 50 coins weighed approximately 0.5kg, this means that there were about 60,000 people classified as wealthy at this time. However, it is clear that the available wealth was in no sense spread evenly across the population. Small groups of influential land-owners and merchants lived lives of luxury and splendour, but the rights and needs of the poor were largely ignored. The concept of brotherhood on which the nation had been founded seemed no longer to have any significance.

Small farmers had suffered greatly during the Aramean attacks of the previous century. A couple of years of drought forced them to mortgage their land to pay for seed, and further bad harvests prompted the money-lenders to evict rather than help them, so that unemployment and homelessness were widespread. The growing landless class created in this way, saw little of the nation's renewed prosperity and society came to be characterized by extremes of wealth and poverty. This situation was worsened by the partiality and greed of the judiciary; it was very difficult for the poor to get justice in any dispute with wealthier countrymen. Judah seems to have taken a little longer than Israel to reach a similar depth of corruption but the situation of the two Hebrew kingdoms was ultimately very similar.

MORAL AND RELIGIOUS CONDITIONS

From a religious point of view, however, things were apparently going very well. In both Israel and Judah the worship of Yahweh was popular, feast days were kept, all the prescribed rituals were followed, sacrifices were offered with great ceremonial and regardless of expense. People in general interpreted the economic recovery as a sign of God's blessing. There was a pervasive mood of optimism, and a confident conviction that God would protect his chosen people in all circumstances.

However, in all this they were treating Yahweh, the Almighty Creator, as if he were an idol or a baal to be pacified by the right kind of religious ritual. They forgot that he was a righteous and jealous God who would not tolerate the worship of other gods and who made moral demands on his people. Alongside their worship of Yahweh, idolatry was rampant, and the religious ceremonies were superficial, having little or no effect on everyday behaviour. There was a total disregard for God's commands and oppression, injustice, dishonesty and immorality characterized both kingdoms.

Such was the state of affairs when the eighth century prophets lived and worked.

CHAPTER 6

Amos

OUTLINE

AMOS THE MAN

All we know about Amos is contained in his book and even there he personally is referred to only twice. 1:1 tells us that he came from Judah, where he was a shepherd at Tekoa — a village about 12 miles south of Jerusalem situated on the edge of the plateau and overlooking the Dead Sea and the Judean wilderness. According to 7:14 he also took care of sycamore-fig trees. This could mean either a) that he was a poor farm-hand who needed to eke out his meagre wages by also working in a sycamore-fig (or fig-mulberry) orchard; or b) that he was a Tekoan notable, a wealthy man who either owned or managed both herds of sheep or cattle and also orchards. The first of these

possibilities would explain why he identified so readily
with the poor people of Israel, but in fact the terminology
used makes the latter more likely. The word used for
shepherd occurs elsewhere in the Old Testament only in
2 Kings 3:4 where it refers to the large scale breeding
programme of Mesha, king of Moab. It seems probable
that it was as Amos travelled to organize the export of his
produce to Israel — Bethel could be reached in a day's
journey from Tekoa and Samaria in two — that he saw
and was shocked by the extent of the social injustice and
oppression and was challenged by God to speak out about
it.

In what sense was Amos a prophet? In 7:14 Amaziah,
the priest of Bethel, appears to acknowledge that Amos
had a prophetic ministry but insists that as a native of
Judah, Amos should return to Judah to deliver his prophecies. In reply Amos explained that he was not a professional prophet and was not trained in any prophetic
school. He was an ordinary man with an ordinary job who
had been called by God to deliver a particular message in
a particular situation. Amaziah's demand that he should
go back to Judah and prophesy there was therefore
completely unacceptable. His commission was to bring
God's word to Israel. It was in that context that he was a
prophet and Amaziah's protests could not take away that
responsibility.

Amos received his message for Israel sometime during
the reigns of Uzziah in Judah and Jeroboam in Israel, 'two
years before the earthquake'. This earthquake in Uzziah's
reign must have been a momentous event as it is also
referred to in Zechariah 14:5 but we cannot date it more
precisely. The times when Jeroboam was sole ruler of
Israel and Uzziah was sole ruler of Judah amount to about
twenty years from c. 770–750 BC, and most scholars would
date Amos' prophetic activity around 760 BC. The book is
not just an account of one long speech but seems to consist
of a number of separate oracles, possibly delivered in a
number of different places. We know that Amos prophesied at Bethel, but there are references which may indi-

cate that he also spoke out at Samaria (3:9–12; 4:1–3; 6:1) and possibly at Gilgal (4:4; 5:5). We cannot be certain about this, but the period when he was delivering his prophecies is usually assumed to be fairly short; perhaps a few weeks or a few months.

THE COMPILATION OF THE BOOK

Some time elapsed between Amos delivering his prophecies and their compilation in written form, as this cannot have happened until after the earthquake mentioned in 1:1. However, we can only speculate about the circumstances in which the oracles were written up. Amos was the first of the 'writing prophets' and there was no apparent tradition of written prophecies. An indication of this is found in 1:1. The introduction refers to 'The words of Amos', rather than the 'The word of the Lord that came to Amos' which became the more formal norm later on. Possibly, Amos was deported from Israel and edited his messages on returning to Tekoa. The suggestion is sometimes made that a group of disciples followed Amos about and later put his prophecies on record, but there is no evidence for this and it seems more likely that Amos himself was responsible for the written form.

The book consists almost entirely of accusations and prophecies of judgment, emphasized in chapters 7 and 8 by a number of visionary illustrations. The only other types of material are the narrative in 7:10–17 and the prophecy of restoration and hope in 9:11–15.

Because of its different form 7:10–17 has sometimes been regarded as a later editorial addition, but it could equally well be seen as the context around which the book is structured and certainly helps to make sense of the whole. Similarly it has been argued that the message of hope in chapter 9 is so out of character with the rest of the book that it is impossible to envisage that the verses could have been produced by the same author. It is therefore assumed to be a later addition, perhaps from the post-exilic period. However, Amos regarded the inhabitants of Israel as part of the whole covenant people of God, which also included Judah, and he was aware that God was sovereign in mercy as well as in judgment. If one accepts the possibility of a predictive element in prophecy, then this picture of hope can easily be seen not as a restoration of the northern kingdom which Amos recognized was doomed, but as a 'remnant' hope for God's people through Judah. The reference in verse 11 to 'David's fallen tent' would support this. Wolff's comment here is worth noting: 'The conclusion of the book witnesses to the assurance that the proclamation of Amos concerning the end of Israel was not God's last word' (p. 354, *Joel and Amos*, Fortress Press, 1977).

THE MESSAGE OF AMOS

Amos appears to have been horrified at the way in which the lifestyle of the Israelite people was so completely opposed to all that he knew of God and of the covenant. This sense of shock and horror underlies much of what Amos says; indeed one can almost overhear his inner dialogue. 'How can they possibly behave in such a way and still think that God will bless them? Have they not even begun to realize what God is like and what he expects of them as his people? Don't they realize what they are doing, don't they understand that God is bound to judge them? If they don't realize it then I must tell them'. Thus Amos's message is basically one of judgment on Israel, aptly expressed by Amaziah in 7:11: 'Jeroboam will die by the sword, and Israel will surely go into exile away from their native land.'

However there is more to Amos than Amaziah's summary implies. His message of judgment must be seen in the overall context of a message from Yahweh, about Yahweh and about Yahweh's relationship with and attitude to Israel and also to other nations. We can attempt to sum up Amos's multifaceted teaching under five headings:

1 *Proclamation of God*

Although Amos pronounced God's condemnation of Israel's injustice and immorality he did not perceive God only as an unbending judge. The prophet's awareness of God as the loving sovereign Lord undergirds the whole book and goes far beyond his conviction that sin will be dealt with. Amos presents God as:

a) *Creator and Lord of Creation.* Amos teaches explicitly that God created the whole earth, including such overwhelming features as the mountains, the wind, and the heavens. He takes it for granted that God has both the right and the power to use all the forces of creation for his own purposes (4:7; 5:8–9; 9:5–6).

b) *Lord of the Nations.* This conviction is linked to the recognition of God as Creator. Some of the detailed implications are examined below.

c) *Unique.* When Amos says (6:8), 'The Sovereign LORD has sworn by himself', this is because there was no one else for Yahweh to swear by! Amos used to be regarded as the founder of 'ethical monotheism', i.e. the belief that there is only one God and that he demands ethical behaviour. Amos certainly teaches this, but it is now more commonly accepted that this is not new teaching but based on the covenant tradition.

d) *Active in History.* God's work did not stop at creation; he continues to be involved in the lives of human beings. This is a constant assumption throughout the book, which includes descriptions of what God has already done and predictions of what he will continue to do (2:9–11; 6:8,11, 14).

e) *Just and Righteous.* One reason why Amos so strongly condemns injustice is that it cuts right across the nature of God who is totally just in his dealings with humanity and absolutely righteous (5:14–15; 24).

f) *Holy.*   Another very significant aspect of God's nature is his holiness. This concept includes righteousness but also involves a kind of awesome apartness reflecting absolute purity. The immoral and unjust behaviour of the covenant people profanes God's holy name (2:7). Again, Amos' knowledge and understanding of God is the basis of his condemnation of the people of Israel.

g) *Making demands.* God has created all people as responsible and as such he makes demands on them (see #2 below). What he requires from all mankind he expects also from Israel but they are especially responsible for living out the covenant, not only by obeying covenant laws, but also by living in such a way that God is adequately represented.

h) *Committed to Israel.* The demands God makes on Israel are not one-sided. God relates to Israel, sharing himself with them and acting on their behalf. (2:9–11; 3:7; 5:14).

i) *Loving and caring.* This can be seen both in God's particular concern for the weak and the poor and also in the descriptions of his mercy. 7:1–6 is a clear illustration of this. God must judge Israel's sin but in his love and his mercy he gives them chance after chance to repent.

2   *God and the nations*

Given that the heart of Amos's message is judgment on Israel, it is fascinating to see how emphatically he also affirms that God is concerned with all nations. In 1:3 – 2:5 judgment is proclaimed on seven nations that surround Israel. This section underlines the responsibility of mankind in general towards God and his expectations of them. Each oracle begins with the same formula: 'For three sins of . . . , even for four, I will not turn back my wrath.' This makes it clear that it was not a single isolated event that attracted God's judgment; like Israel, the nations were given plenty of leeway. In each case one major sin is mentioned, perhaps the one that eventually clinched the judgment against them.

Most of the crimes referred to occur in warfare or international relations. These judgments assume that there is an absolute morality required from all men, quite apart from the specific requirements of the covenant law which applied only to Israel and Judah. It is taken for granted that humankind possesses a built-in awareness of right and wrong. In each case, the punishment involves war; fire is also mentioned. There may be some reference here to the expansion of the Assyrian Empire and the battles resulting from this.

The sin of the Arameans, represented by Damascus, was brutal behaviour. God will not tolerate barbarism and unrestrained cruelty even in war. Nations which engage in such conduct will eventually, meet their doom. The twentieth century concept of 'war-crimes' is very relevant to this section, which could be seen as the basis for international agreements like the Geneva convention. The Philistines are condemned for being slave-traders. It was normal to take captives in war and sometimes to use them as slaves, but here the captives were sold to a third party. Yahweh will not tolerate human beings being treated as mere objects. The crime of Tyre was also slave-trading, made worse in this case because it involved breaking a covenant treaty. Edom, Ammon and Moab were also condemned for unbrotherly behaviour, for brutality and for ignoring the deepest sensibilities of captives.

Only in the case of Judah is the designated crime against God rather than against human beings. The principle seems to be that those who have received greater knowledge and revelation will be judged to be more responsible. However, Amos was clearly convinced that whatever gods the nations may acknowledge, in fact they are all subjects of Yahweh, the sovereign Lord of creation of history and all are obligated to live according to his standards.

It is not only as judge that God relates to the nations.

In 6:2, Israel is told to consider the nations and to realize that she has no right to assume that she is in herself more significant than they are. 9:7 even more remarkably suggests that God has been no less involved in other people-movements than he was in Israel's exodus from Egypt. Israel had assumed that the covenant with Yahweh made her the 'foremost nation' (6:1), but any view about the uniqueness of Israel must take into account God's involvement with the whole world.

3   *Warning and challenge to Israel about injustice*

The primary factor which convinced Amos that God wanted hm to prophesy to Israel seems to have been the blatant examples of injustice that he saw as he travelled about the land. Horrified himself, he began to sense something of God's horror at these social crimes which indicated a refusal to take God seriously and to recognize men and women as in the image of God. The nations deserved condemnation for 'war crimes' against other countries. But as H. W. Wolff puts it, 'Israel's "war crimes" are acts committed by the powerful in oppressing the poor among their own people' (*Joel and Amos*, Fortress Press, p. 165). Amos saw much that appalled him and we can identify several areas of particular concern.

a) *Business and Trade.* The covenant was based on the principle that Israel was a family where the stronger would help the weaker and where it should be impossible for a vast gulf to develop between the rich and the poor. But this was dependent on goodwill and in practice it was possible to keep within the strict limits of the law and still behave in a way which was oppressive and in Amos's view morally indefensible. This was how the wealthy land-owners were behaving.

Apparently the 'needy', those who ought to bring out the mercy and charity of others, were being sold into slavery for debts as trivial as the cost of a pair of sandals (2:6). Heavy interest payments were exacted and even grain which was needed not only for food, but for the next year's crop was taken, so that the poor were deliberately being further impoverished (5:11). Dishonest trading, in which weights were altered or floor sweepings added to the wheat sacks as ballast, was also apparently common, usually at the expense of the poor (8:5–6). Such profiteering at the expense of human dignity was abhorrent to Amos and to Yahweh.

b) *The Legal System.* Not only did they 'trample on the heads of the poor', they also 'denied justice to the oppressed' (2:7). It appears that the wealthy, or at least the arrogant and brutal, found it easier to get their 'rights' in court than did the poor (5:10,12). This cut right across the basic principles of covenant law which explicitly protected the poor and forbade any kind of favouritism (Exodus 23:6–8; Deuteronomy 16:19–20).

c) *Self-Indulgence.* Amos denounced not only those who were obviously unjust, but also those whose life-style showed selfishness and lack of concern for the welfare of their poorer fellow countrymen. The description of wealthy society women as 'fat cows' (4:1), was as insulting then as it sounds today, but Amos saw it as appropriate! Cows are interested only in their own desires and so were these women. Their own luxuries mattered more to them than the basic human needs of others, and they would happily use oppression to support their own greed. Such an attitude — differentiating between groups of people as being of different value — is totally unacceptable to God. But these people who owned two houses when others had none (3:15), whose lifestyle was luxurious and even dissipated, and who imagined they were 'first' in the land (6:1), would end up having priority only in the deportation (6:7).

4   *Warning and challenge to Israel about the cultus*

Amos condemned the cultus, the way in which the

Israelites practised their religion, on two grounds. Firstly their worship was syncretistic; it had become idolatrous and included various pagan customs, including such things as sacred prostitution (2:7–8, 12;5:26). But the main focus of his criticism was that their religion had no effect at all on their life-style and was thus sheer hypocrisy. They may be very zealous in keeping feasts and in bringing sacrifices but if these were not accompanied by justice and righteousness in their daily lives then far from pleasing God, their religious practices were hateful to him. Worship in Israel was supposed to stem out of their covenant with God, it was a means of strengthening their relationship with him and of reflecting the love between Yahweh and all his people. However, if Israel's national life so contradicted the covenant relationship then their worship was at best totally pointless and at worst increased their sin by treating God as if he could be manipulated (4:4–5; 5:4–6, 21–27).

5   *Announcement of judgment*

God's judgment is not indiscriminate. It was clear to Amos that those who did live according to the covenant, those who were truly seeking God (5:4), would survive. What makes his book so full of sadness is that he fully recognized the extent of the nations' corruption, and knew that the number of true believers was pathetically small. Realizing how unlikely it was that the rest would really repent, he threatened judgment, not in a spirit of gloating but as a last ditch attempt to help more of them realize what they were actually doing, repent, and hence avoid the judgment.

The nature of the judgment is aptly summed up by Amaziah in 7:11: 'Jeroboam will die by the sword and Israel will surely go into exile'. Israel had longed for the 'day of the Lord' (5:18). They looked forward to it as the time when God would judge the nations, as he intervened on Israel's behalf; the time when Israel would be proclaimed as sovereign over other nations. Amos tried to jolt the Israelites out of their false sense of security, making it clear that this 'day' was something to be feared, since God would judge Israel also and because of their sin, he would destroy them. As Amos describes this destruction, he evokes pictures of darkness, famine, war, weeping and wailing, earthquake, staggering and mourning. We are left in no doubt of its inevitability. The message of judgment is not the last word, and for those who hear and heed the message 9:11–15 provide great hope. But 9:10 is clear: 'All the sinners among my people will die by the sword, all those who say "Disaster will not overtake or meet us".'

TASTERS IN AMOS

1   *Amos 5:4–6*

This is what the Lord says to the house of Israel: 4
    'Seek me and live;
do not seek Bethel,   5
    do not go to Gilgal,
    do not journey to Beersheba.
For Gilgal will surely go into exile,
    and Bethel will be reduced to nothing.'
Seek the LORD and live,
    or he will sweep through the house of Joseph like a fire;
    it will devour, and Bethel will have no-one to quench it.

In verse 4 the call to 'seek God and live' shows explicitly that repentance and forgiveness are possible. In verse 5 it is made quite clear that seeking God is not the same thing at all as visiting Bethel or Gilgal or any other of the shrines. Much 'religion' went on at Bethel and Gilgal, as is shown in 4:4, but the implication in both these verses is that because of the nation's syncretism and their toleration of blatant injustices true worship at these shrines had become impossible and therefore they are to be completely shunned. The situation is desperate; the only alternative to seeking God and hence obtaining life is total destruction. Amos cares deeply that his hearers escape this fate, and these verses with their pleading tone reveal how much God himself cares. But if seeking God is not the same as 'being religious', what does it involve? The rest of the chapter shows that it certainly entails practical concern for the poor and maintaining justice in the courts. One cannot seek God without also seeking good (5:14).

2   *Amos 8:1–6*

This is what the Sovereign LORD showed me: a basket
    of ripe fruit.
'What do you see, Amos?' he asked.   2
    'A basket of ripe fruit,' I answered.
Then the LORD said to me, 'The time is ripe for my
    people Israel; I will spare them no longer.
'In that day,' declares the Sovereign LORD, 'the   3
    songs in the temple will turn to wailing. Many,
    many bodies — flung everywhere! Silence!'

Hear this, you who trample the needy   4
    and do away with the poor of the land,
saying,   5
'When will the New Moon be over that we may sell
    grain,
    and the Sabbath be ended that we may market
    wheat?'—
    skimping the measure, boosting the price
    and cheating with dishonest scales,
buying the poor with silver   6
    and the needy for a pair of sandals,
    selling even the sweepings with the wheat.'

The messages in Amos are not all presented as a series of arguments; several times they are prefaced by a God-given vision picturing the state that Israel is in. Here the vision is simply of a basket of ripe summer fruit, perhaps with the implication that they are over-ripe. (Summer fruit had to be eaten or dried immediately as it went bad very quickly.) The word for 'summer fruit' and the word for 'end' sound very similar in Hebrew and Amos uses this word-play to make a point. NIV brings this out by translating 'The end has come' for Israel as 'The time is ripe.' The judgment will come and will be as irrevocable as the deterioration of over-ripe fruit. That this really is the end, that it involves death, is brought out very dramatically in verse 3. The call for 'silence' is not a description but a command. There is no longer anything more to be said.

Verse 4 probably starts a separate section but there is a clear connection of thought and the same Hebrew word is used in '. . . you who bring the poor of the land to an end'. Amos is telling them to look out for their own end! The focus of interest and the ground for condemnation are once more injustice and oppression, expressed generally in verse 4 and more specifically in vv5–6, where irreligion also features. These people are not in the least interested in the proper use of the Sabbath or 'New Moon' (a monthly festival when, as on the Sabbath no business was conducted). They are so interested in making money that in spite of an apparent religiosity, they cannot wait to get on with their profiteering. This money-making attitude would in itself be bad enough, but it has led them also into cheating and oppression. It seems as if the whole society has gone bad. No wonder Amos sees them like rotting fruit, and no wonder God proclaims judgment on them.

AMOS FOR TODAY

The message of Amos for Israel in the eighth century BC is fairly clear, but what is the relevance of Amos for today? What principles can we identify which still apply, both to individual Christians who see themselves as having a personal relationship with God and therefore as particularly responsible to him, and to society in general? We could mention many individual points, but four main areas deserve special investigation.

Understanding God

God has not changed and we do well to heed what Amos teaches us about him. God is still the unique Lord of all creation, he is still active in history, still merciful, loving and caring, still holy, just and righteous, still makes demands both on his own people and on mankind in general and will still judge all those who fail to meet those demands. Certainly the coming of Jesus and the gospel make a difference to our understanding of God, how sin can be dealt with and how God's demands can be met. But to understand God as Amos did brings both a great joy, that we are able to relate to him and to trust in his love and continuing faithfulness to us, and a great challenge, that we live our lives in a way that reflects him to others and that we explain to the world what God is like, how seeking him will bring them life and neglecting his requirements will bring death.

Worship

The Old Testament law has very strict regulations about the form that Israel's worship should take. Amos clearly teaches that even keeping these regulations in exact detail, bringing all the proper gifts and sacrifices, using the best songs and music, taking part in all the feasts, did not mean that true worship was taking place. One of the things that God detests most is hypocrisy, and worship of God that is not accompanied by a life-style expressing his nature is always hypocritical. 'Religion' on its own is never enough. Worship may be lively and enjoyable or solemn and dignified; both can be good but we cannot judge the spirituality of a church simply by the pattern of its worship services. Whatever our tradition there is a danger that our worship may degenerate into nothing more than irrelevant words and actions. Amos provides us with a strong warning against this.

Personal Life-Style

What then does Amos tell us about the kind of life-style that enables us to worship God properly? In general terms, God's people must be honest, just, caring, and not self-indulgent. Specifically we must avoid using bribes of any kind or manipulating people or circumstances in order to benefit ourselves at the expense of others. We must not be involved in cheating of any kind. We must not make excessive charges for rent or interest which would force people into poverty or homelessness. (Even when the market will bear it, and if our present tenants cannot pay, others will?)

We are to treat all people properly, giving them the value they deserve as individuals created by God in his image and never assuming that certain groups have more rights or more value than others. We must shun all kinds of shady or oppressive practices. One cannot imagine either Amos or the God he served having much time for the kind of arguments that we so often hear today; 'I am acting within my strict legal rights in doing this', or, 'Everybody does it, it's part of the system and you can't change it' or even, 'You can't survive in business without this kind of thing happening'. Wealth and luxury are not wrong in themselves but self-indulgence that ignores the needs of others clearly is.

Political Involvement

Obviously our first priority is to get our own personal life-style sorted out, to identify any areas in our lives that would shock a modern-day Amos and deal with them. But

Amos makes it clear that God makes righteous demands upon all societies, even when they pay no allegiance at all to him. Particularly in a democratic society where we do have a voice and a vote, we have a responsibility to try and ensure that our nation is structured in a way that is just, that gives people proper value and is not oppressive in any way. We must make certain that our legal system ensures justice is available for all regardless of their wealth or status; that the taxation system and the business community are organized in such a way that if there is any bias it is towards moving wealth from the rich to the poor and not the other way around; that people are not driven further into poverty because they are unable to keep up excessive interest payments; and that these same principles are applied also in relationships with other nations. That our own society may have a very good record in some of these areas does not take away its responsibility to act in the others.

Each one of us must ask whether God is calling us, perhaps like Amos from a very ordinary job, to speak out about particular instances of injustice, hypocrisy or oppression whether in the church or in society in general.

CHAPTER 7

Hosea

OUTLINE

HOSEA: THE MAN AND HIS FAMILY

We know very little about Hosea's background except that his father's name was Beeri. His prophecies are directed almost entirely towards Israel (often referred to in his book as Ephraim, after the largest tribe) and it is almost certain that he himself came from the northern kingdom. In fact, Hosea is the only prophet actually from Israel whose writings have survived. It has been suggested that his detailed knowledge of baking (7:4–8) could indicate that this was his trade but he also uses similar imagery from farming (10:11–13 11:3), and one could see that as his background, or he may have been a professional prophet.

His use of language and the breadth of his knowledge show him to have been well-educated.

1:1 tells us that Hosea worked as a prophet sometime between 780 BC and 692 BC. The only Israelite king mentioned here is Jeroboam II, who died in 746 BC, but there are specific references to events that happened after this (5:13; 10:14). It is likely that most of his messages were given from about 755–722 BC, in the time leading up to the fall of Samaria and the end of the northern kingdom.

There are problems in sorting out exactly what happened in Hosea's own family but it is clear that his home life was to all intents and purposes a disaster. He was instructed to marry a woman who was either sexually promiscuous when he married her, or was destined to become so at a later date. The text seems clear, but some see difficulties in accepting that God may have commanded Hosea to act in a way that was clearly contrary to his law. It may be that Gomer's promiscuity was, at least at first, associated with the fertility rites of the Baal religion and indicates how far Israel had moved from keeping their covenant with Yahweh, their own covenant Lord. Gomer bore three children while she was married to Hosea. Their names were chosen to illustrate God's judgment on Israel and those of the latter two may also reflect Hosea's growing suspicions that he might not be the father.

In the end Gomer ran away and apparently became a prostitute. Some while later, while she was still living with another man but having no more status than a slave, Hosea was told to buy her back, love her again and restore her to the status of his wife. Gomer is not named in chapter 3 and it has been suggested that this portion of the book refers to a second adulterous woman, but the link with chapter 1 seems clear. Whatever the exact details, Hosea's own life gave him a deep understanding both of the meaning of love and commitment in a relationship and also of the suffering involved when trust is betrayed. Because of his own experiences, Hosea could identify with and explain something of the way in which God suffered as a result of his relationship with Israel.

Having said that, it is right to point out that Hosea was able to love his wife, even though she was adulterous, because he had already recognized that God still loved the people of Israel even though they rejected him and preferred to turn to the questionable benefits of the fertility cults (3:1).

THE BOOK

Chapter 3 is a first person autobiographical account and chapter 1 a third person narrative account of these events in Hosea's life. The whole of the rest of the book consists of prophetic messages which were apparently originally delivered in oral form. Most of these can be described as judgment oracles, although both within them and elsewhere we find proclamations of God's constant love, and laments over Israel's unfaithfulness. Hosea portrays a remarkable depth of feeling. It is worth reading through the book at one sitting just to appreciate the magnitude of God's love for his people and the extent of the sadness and the suffering that he feels because of their unfaithfulness, as well as the anger at their sin.

There are possible signs of editorial activity in Hosea and a small number of verses are disputed, but there is general agreement with the view of J. L. Mays that 'very little material that did not originate with Hosea has been added in the formation and use of the book' (*Hosea* SCM p. 16). Some Israelites who still maintained their covenant faith in Yahweh escaped to Judah about the time of the fall of Samaria. It seems likely that they took copies of Hosea's prophecies with them and that this material was edited and arranged in book form very soon afterwards. Even if Hosea himself was not one of those who travelled to Judah and was not involved in this process of editing, it was certainly done on a basis of contact with Hosea or people who knew him and valued his work.

Chapters 1–3, with their concentration on Hosea's own life, serve as an introduction to the whole. It may be that the rest of the material is organized chronologically, in the order Hosea gave the messages, but it may have been arranged according to content. Chapters 4–11 in general present a message of judgment and chapters 12–14 a message of hope, with the different oracles grouped together according to theme or linked by key-words.

THE MESSAGE OF HOSEA

Amos was a business man and an activist. God used his particular gifts and personality to challenge Israel about their behaviour and the need for them as God's people to reflect God's justice and God's righteousness in their own lives. Hosea had a different perspective; his outlook was dominated by the anguish of his own family life and the central concern of his prophecy was to portray the anguish of God at the way his relationship with Israel had developed; at the way in which they had deliberately rejected him and chosen instead to follow the Baal cult. Hosea's central idea is that real religion is relationship with God and therefore his condemnation is primarily directed towards the nation's idolatry and irreligion rather than its immorality and oppression. Perhaps because the covenant between God and Israel is so much on his mind, Hosea does not deal with the responsibilities of other nations.

However, though the perspective may be different, Hosea's basic message is the same as that of Amos. Mankind is responsible to God; sin is serious and will be judged; repentance and restoration are possible and that is what God really wants; failing this, punishment and destruction are inevitable. The major elements of Hosea's teaching are:

1. *Yahweh's Love for Israel*

One thing Hosea was absolutely certain about was the depth and extent of God's love for Israel. Hosea puts his whole heart and soul into convincing his hearers of this and of the fact that it is because of God's great love for them that he minds so much about their sin. God's love is constant and unchanging. He has looked after them and blessed them ever since he first brought them out of Egypt and entered into a covenant relationship with them (2:14–15; 11:1; 13:4–5). Even when they became deeply corrupted, God's deepest desire was to heal them and restore them (7:1; 11:8–9). God's gracious love meant that there was hope for future salvation for any who did respond to his love (11:10–12; 14:4–9).

One of Hosea's most significant illustrations was his portrayal of God as Israel's husband. Other prophets tend to avoid this kind of sex-related imagery because of misunderstandings which could arise from the role of such imagery in the Canaanite fertility cults. But Hosea did not hesitate to take the imagery and motifs that had become so common because of Israel's preoccupation with Baalism and to transform them for his own purposes. He totally rejected everything to do with Baalism, including its use of sex in cultic and magical fertility rites, but he still used marriage to stress the moral responsibilities within the covenant relationship. Yahweh had bound himself to Israel as a husband to a wife, and he loved her and kept on loving her. Even when she spurned the covenant, committing spiritual adultery, he still sought her out and was willing to restore her to her original status (2:2 – 3:1).

But even such a dramatic picture as this was not enough for Hosea to portray every aspect of God's love. He is also seen as a father lovingly watching over the first tottering steps of his small son (11:1ff); as a doctor carefully healing the wounds of his patients (7:1; 11:3; 14:4); and as a shepherd protecting, feeding and supplying the needs of his flock (11:4; 13:5).

Yet God's love is not just expressed in his care for Israel, nor is it simply something that makes him a 'soft touch' for them to manipulate at will. Rather it takes them seriously as people and allows them the dignity of taking responsibility for their own decisions even when these necessitate punishment. Through Hosea, God pleads with them to repent but the decision has to be their own (7:1–2; 11:8–11). Again, God's love is not undemanding, it seeks a response from the loved one.

Hosea himself had grasped and wanted the Israelites to understand that God's love was not simply an 'objective' or 'abstract' aspect of his character. Yahweh was a person and he was fully and personally involved in his relationship with them. Angered by their sin, he was also deeply hurt by their rejection of his love, and suffered great distress because they refused to turn from the path which would inevitably lead to their destruction.

2. *The Requirements of Relationship*

The people of Israel had taken their relationship with Yahweh for granted, imagining that they could negotiate or even dictate the conditions under which this relationship would continue. But God is both sovereign and holy and relationship with him can exist only on his terms. Firstly their allegiance to him must be total and exclusive. This was made quite clear in the original covenant and Hosea's imagery reinforces the point. To worship other gods or to trust in the power of other nations is to break the terms of the covenant and is as destructive to the relationship with God as adultery in a marriage (2:2; 5:13; 11:5–7). God cannot allow his own people to depend on or to serve anyone else, he demands wholehearted loyalty and faithfulness.

Secondly, relationship requires knowledge. It is impossible to relate to somebody you know nothing about, which is why God's people need to study God's word in order to discover what God is like and what God requires. If they are to 'know him', they must know something about him. It was the responsibility of the priests to make sure that the people did know about God and they therefore carried a great deal of blame for the defection of the people (4:6–9).

Thirdly, if a nation is to be the people of God, then their

behaviour must reflect the character of God. They must show righteousness and justice, love and compassion (2:20; 12:6) and in general they must be obedient to God's covenant law.

Finally, if the relationship broken by the sin of the people is ever to be restored, which is what God longs for, then there must be repentance and a clear turning away from their previous way of life. This repentance must be real, involving a change of heart and evidenced by a change in behaviour. It was certainly not enough merely to bring a few extra sacrifices to keep God happy. (5:4; 6:1–6).

3. *Israel's Failure*

The form of the whole of chapters 4–14 is linked with that of a court case. The charge against Israel is that although they continue to live in the land and to expect the benefits of the covenant, they are no longer keeping their part of it, no longer meeting God's requirements. 'There is no faithfulness, no love, no acknowledgment of God in the land. There is only cursing, lying and murder, stealing and adultery, they break all bounds and bloodshed follows bloodshed' (4:2). They engage in prostitution, idolatry, immorality, arrogance and hypocrisy (2:8; 4:10–13; 5:7; 8:2–6; 12:7–8). In fact, rejection of God and disobedience to him is so universal that the surprising thing about Hosea's message is not his proclaiming God's thoroughly deserved judgment on them, but his insistence that God, far from writing them off, still loves them and yearns for them to repent and return to a renewed relationship with him.

The imagery Hosea uses to describe faithless Israel is almost as varied as that which he uses to describe God's love. Israel is not only like an adulterous wife (2:2–5) and an unresponsive child (11:1–3) but also like a stubborn cow (4:16), a sick person (5:13), an unturned cake, burnt on one side and raw on the other (7:8), or like a foolish bird (7:11–12).

4.   The Judgment and the Punishment

In a powerful and profound way Hosea conveys the
tension between God's desire to heal and restore Israel,
and the reality of his holiness and his judgment which
means that sin must and will be dealt with; it cannot and
will not be ignored. Because they had broken the covenant
God would give them names which Hosea symbolically
gave to his children. One was named Jezreel, 'because I
will soon punish the house of Jehu [the royal family] for
the massacre at Jezreel and I will put an end to the people
of Israel', a second child was called 'Not-loved' and a third
'Not-my-people' (2:4, 6, 9). Hosea explains that Yahweh
wanted the best for Israel and in the covenant he provides
the way in which they can receive that 'best'. Nevertheless,
he will not override their capacity as human beings to
make responsible decisions. If they decide against the
covenant then the consequences of that decision will be
allowed to stand.

Because they had trusted in the rituals of the fertility
cults rather than in the God of Creation, the blessings of
fertility that God himself had given them would be taken
away. They would suffer from drought, famine, plague
and childlessness (2:9–13; 9:2–7, 11–13; 10:8). Because they
had trusted in political alliances with pagan nations and
in the intrigues of a corrupt monarchy rather than in God
and his law, every aspect of their political existence would
fail. Alliances would provide no support and they would
suffer devastating military defeats and humiliating political
disintegration. The nation would go into exile. (5:8–9,13–14;
7:9–12, 16; 8:3, 10; 9:3, 6, 15; 10:3–10; 11:5–6).

All these disasters are presented by Hosea both as the
natural consequences of their own actions, — they have
sown the wind and will indeed reap the whirlwind (8:7)
— and also as the direct action of God in judgment. They
could have related to Yahweh as their husband and their
father but because of their sin he will be to them like an
insect causing decay (5:12), a hunter (7:12) or a beast of
prey (5:14; 13:7–8) seeking not to support but to destroy
(13:9).

5. *Restoration and Hope*

If Israel continued on the path they had chosen, then destruction was inevitable. But Hosea took great pains to explain that there was another possibility. If Israel or any individuals within Israel would repent and turn to God then the future for them would be very different. There would be a day of restoration when Israel would again become God's true wife (2:14–16). Although the worship of Baal had destroyed the old covenant, yet God in his mercy would initiate a new covenant, a permanent one where God himself would provide peace, security and prosperity and Israel would respond by fully acknowledging him. This new relationship would affect all areas of life even including the natural environment (2:17–23). Although the specific term is not used here, this teaching has very clear links with Jeremiah's prophecy about the 'new covenant' (Jeremiah 31:31ff).

Hosea does not seem to have had much hope that Israel as a whole would respond to God's loving overtures, but nevertheless he was certain that ultimately God's love would triumph (11:8–11; 14:4–9). It is possible to see this as pointing forward to the New Testament description of God's love revealed in Jesus. Sin can be defeated, not by ignoring or side-stepping it but by finding a way to deal with it.

TASTERS IN HOSEA

1. *Hosea 5:15 – 6:6*

'Then I will go back to my place [15]
  until they admit their guilt.
And they will seek my face;
  in their misery they will earnestly seek me.'

'Come, let us return to the LORD. [1]
He has torn us to pieces but he will heal us;
  he has injured us but he will bind up our wounds.

After two days he will revive us;   2
  on the third day he will restore us,
  that we may live in his presence.
Let us acknowledge the LORD; let us press on to   3
  acknowledge him.
As surely as the sun rises, he will appear;
  he will come to us like the winter rains,
  like the spring rains that water the earth.'

'What can I do with you, Ephraim?   4
What can I do with you, Judah?
Your love is like the morning mist,
  like the early dew that disappears.
Therefore I cut you in pieces with my prophets,   5
  I killed you with the words of my mouth;
  my judgments flashed like lightning upon you.
For I desire mercy, not sacrifice,   6
  and acknowledgment of God rather than burnt
  offerings.

Chapter 5 describes God disciplining Israel and in verse
15 we see him awaiting their response. The first three
verses of chapter 6 make it appear that God's action has
succeeded and that Israel has responded by turning to
God and acknowledging his lordship. The words used are
exactly right: what the nation needed above all else was
to 'know' the Lord. But the rest of the chapter makes it
clear that this response is rooted in complacency, not
repentance. Israel hopes for a quick solution to her problems; if they manage to get on the right side of God he
will sort things out in two or three days! Perhaps they are
using an established 'Song of Repentance', a commonly
known hymn which was used at such times of national
disaster.

Verses 4–6 show that God is not deceived. He is only
too well aware that their response is not heartfelt; it will
vanish as quickly as the dew or an early morning mist. But
the picture is still of God trying to find a way in which he
can get through to Israel. He has tried using prophets to
batter down their opposition to him but even when Israel

has taken notice they have simply increased their support for cultic ritual. But God wants 'mercy', perhaps better translated here as 'steadfast love' or 'devotion', and knowledge of him, not just religious rituals. Hosea is not condemning sacrifice as such here, but he is denouncing sacrifice made, not in a spirit of humble obedience but in order to manipulate God.

2. *Hosea 14:1–8*

Return, O Israel, to the LORD your God.
　Your sins have been your downfall!
Take words with you and return to the LORD.   2
Say to him: 'Forgive all our sins
　and receive us graciously,
　that we may offer the fruit of our lips.
Assyria cannot save us;   3
　we will not mount war-horses.
We will never again say 'Our gods'
　to what our own hands have made,
　for in you the fatherless find compassion.'

I will heal their waywardness   4
　and love them freely,
　for my anger has turned away from them.
I will be like the dew to Israel;   5
　he will blossom like a lily.
Like a cedar of Lebanon
　he will send down his roots;
his young shoots will grow.   6
His splendour will be like an olive tree,
　his fragrance like a cedar of Lebanon.
Men will dwell again in his shade.   7
　He will flourish like the grain.
He will blossom like a vine,
　and his fame will be like the wine from Lebanon.
O Ephraim, what more have I to do with idols?   8
　I will answer him and care for him.
I am like a green pine tree;
　your fruitfulness comes from me.'

The sharp and unexpected change from total doom in chapter 13 to bright hope in chapter 14 has led some commentators to see a different author here. However, if we assume that Hosea did have at least a faint conception of the new covenant ideas later expressed in Jeremiah, and if we see verses 4–9 as God's reply to the repentance called for in verses 1–3, then there is no contradiction and no need to look for a separate author.

'Return' in verse 1 is imperative, a command. The opportunity is there, but Israel must take it. This return has to involve genuine repentance and true worship (v2), the Hebrew literally means 'bulls of our lips': they must offer a sacrifice of praise with words that are sincere. False worship and false dependence on foreign alliances must both be set aside (v3). *If* the command is obeyed and they do return, *then* . . . God's love will come with its healing power and his anger will be set aside. They will be restored to health and wholeness. Verses 5–8 give a delightful picture of what this restored life will be like. All the blessings that they had sought from Baal without effect will be theirs for the taking. They will live in peace and luxury, surrounded by God's love.

HOSEA FOR TODAY

Objectively Hosea provides us with clear evidence about why the northern kingdom of Israel eventually fell. Politically he highlights the increase of Assyrian influence. From the divine viewpoint he emphasizes that God cannot and will not tolerate immorality or idolatry and that our worship must be heartfelt, exclusive and reflected in our lives. But perhaps the most significant lessons from Hosea are in the subjective area of relationship. We learn about love and loyalty, about responsibilities and priorities in a relationship. We learn what it means to belong to and to be committed to another person, whether that be God or another human being, and above all we learn something of the depth of God's love and what it means when he loves us and commits himself to us.

So, if we have grasped Hosea's meaning for the Israelites of his own day, how will that affect our lives?

Being in a covenant relationship with God means that we must be obedient and our behaviour must reflect the fact that we are his. Since he is just, holy, righteous and loving, we must demonstrate this in our own lives. Hosea emphasizes the importance of relationship with God affecting our actions but what he says also transforms our motivation. Any disobedience or sin, is in essence a rejection of God. Because God loves us so much he is deeply hurt by such a rejection. If we love him then we behave rightly not only in order to fulfil our responsibilities but also to avoid hurting the one we love. If we do sin, we can come asking forgiveness and *know* that his love means that he will receive us graciously. Hosea is perhaps the clearest forerunner of the New Testament teaching on this point.

In addition we may ask ourselves if we are expecting God to share our allegiance with some modern equivalent of the Baal cults. We may worship God in theory, but in practice place our trust for security in the stock market, or the welfare state, or a particular political party or an insurance policy or even the local Neighbourhood Watch? None of these things is wrong in itself but if they, or anything else, replace God or even are placed alongside him as recipients of our trust then we are no better than the Israelites.

Finally, an understanding of Hosea's teaching on the love of God is bound to affect our relationships with others. Hosea shows how willing God was to forgive his wayward people and to restore the broken relationship and we see how this enabled Hosea to love his adulterous wife. This must challenge us to test the depth of our own love for friends and family. How much love would we be able to show in situations of hurt and rejection? Hosea teaches that broken relationships can be restored, but gives no glib solution. Such situations are hurtful, even agonizing, and restoration cannot be automatic; it depends on repentance, cleansing, and a commitment to the new start (3:3; 14:2).

Micah

OUTLINE

MICAH, THE MAN

We are not told the name of Micah's father, which could mean that he did not come from an important or well-known family. His town is Moresheth-gath, a small country town on the border with Philistia, situated in a fertile valley, and possibly part of Judah's frontier defence system. Apart from his name and his town we are told little of Micah; the only personal references he makes to himself are in 3:8 and 7:7 which simply show that he was very conscious of his own calling and his relationship with God. He was a skilled communicator and makes effective use of a wide range of styles and of imagery. From his writing we can gather that he was an independent thinker, able and willing to stand against the prophetic trends and fashions of the time. Also we see that he was very much a countryman, believing much of the sin of the people has resulted from corrupt city life. Apparently he moved to Jerusalem and many, if not all, of his oracles were delivered there. But it is interesting to note that his account of the conquering hordes approaching Jerusalem (1:9–16) is from the perspective of someone outside Jerusalem watching the enemy sweep past, whereas Isaiah's account (10:28–34) plainly comes from someone inside the city.

1:1 tells us that Micah prophesied in the southern kingdom of Judah some time between 742 BC and 687 BC. (Throughout the book the general term Israel is used to describe Judah, perhaps now including refugees from the north. The northern kingdom is referred to as Samaria.) Jeremiah quotes Micah 3:12 as being spoken in the reign of Hezekiah (715–687). Broadly speaking it is likely that most of his work was done between 725 and 701 BC; 1:5–6 appears to be before the fall of Samaria in 722 BC and 1:8–20 to refer to the campaign of Sennacherib in 701 BC. He was therefore partly contemporary with Hosea in the north and with Isaiah in Judah and the teachings of both are reflected in his own book.

THE BOOK

Micah is not a single speech delivered at one time; it is a series of fairly loosely connected oracles, so that sometimes there is an abrupt change in the subject matter. Nevertheless the book does have a structure: passages concerned with condemnation and judgment are linked together, as are passages concerned with hope and redemption. In general, chapters 1–3 contain speeches of judgment, chapters 4–5 deal with hope for salvation and chapters 6–7 combine the two, concentrating on Yahweh's relationship with the people, his demands on them and his expectations for them. These prophecies will all have been given independently, but at some stage they have been brought together and arranged so as to form a structured whole.

There is some debate about when the final editing took place and whether additional material was added by an editor other than Micah himself. Such questions may cause concern to people who take a 'high' view of the Bible, as the authoritative word of God. But, since they are concerned with the book as it stands, however it reached its final state, this need not be a problem. In point of fact, almost all scholars assign chapters 1–3 to Micah himself but some feel that the authorship of chapters 4–7 is less certain. They doubt that a prophet who writes so feelingly of doom could also write so gladly of salvation and certainly it is as a prophet of doom that Jeremiah remembers Micah (Jer. 26:18). But all of us know what it is to have deep feelings that change according to the particular issues we are considering. There are also passages which appear to relate to the time during or after the exile. It is suggested that these come from a writer other than the prophet Micah. But this argument is convincing only if one assumes that predictive prophecy is not possible. In addition, 4:1–3, which is repeated in Isaiah 2:1–4, is likely to be a quote from some other source, and questions remain about 7:8–20 which does appear to be written from the perspective of someone about to be released from exile. These passages apart, it is reasonable to regard Micah as the author of everything else in the book.

THE MESSAGE OF MICAH

The heart of Micah's ministry seems to have been the need to teach the people what God was really like. It was in this context that he spoke both of redemption and of judgment. The Judah addressed by Micah was living in exactly the same way as the Israel addressed by Amos. Even the fall of Samaria and the deportation of the Israelites did not change the southerners' confident conviction that in the last resort they would be all right because God would protect them however much they disregarded his commandments. A major part of Micah's task, therefore, was to convince them of the seriousness of sin and the need for repentance. However, Micah in general is more optimistic than either Amos or Hosea. For them, the hope for the future was a possibility open to Israel but one which they did not really expect Israel to take up, at least not as a whole. Micah, perhaps encouraged by the reformation which (though its long term effects were limited) did take place under Hezekiah, confidently expresses the hope that after the judgment a remnant would respond to God and would therefore enjoy the future of which he spoke.

1. *Proclamation of God*

a) *God is holy.* Micah gives us a very dramatic and frightening description of the holy and great God coming down to act in judgment (1:2–4). This picture of the awe-inspiring nature of God is not softened by any reference to the covenant relationship. Micah was well aware of God's love, but knew the people of Judah were totally mistaken in thinking that because God loved them he would overlook their selfishness, corruption and oppression. God is holy and righteous and cannot allow their sin to go unpunished (5:10–15). Sometimes when one aspect of God's nature has been overstressed it is necessary to restore the balance by this kind of strong emphasis.

b) *God is just.* It was possible to bribe the leaders of the nation, whether rulers, prophets or priests, but God cannot be bribed. The rich and powerful will get no special treatment from him; in fact, their schemes to cheat others of land will lead only to the loss of their own land as God makes the punishment fit the crime. (2:3–7; 3:4–5,9–12).

c) *God makes claims on his covenant people.* It is futile for them to expect God to help them if they ignore his demands on them (3:11). Words alone will never satisfy God, his

people must live in a way that matches their words. The
justice, kindness and humility that the covenant speaks of
must be reflected in their everyday lives (6:8).

d) *God loves and forgives.*   The fact that God must and will
punish Israel does not mean any lack of love. He always
has loved them and always will, and even the punishment
is meant to bring them to the place where they can experience God's power to deliver them (2:12–13; 5:3–5; 7:14–15).
God's care stretches even beyond Israel to other nations;
they too must be punished, but there is also a place for
them in the wonderful future time. God cannot ignore sin
but he can forgive the sinner: 7:18–20 which is read by
Jews on the Day of Atonement speaks very powerfully of
God's amazing mercy and forgiveness.

e) *God is in control.*   The world may look as if it is controlled
by foreign nations who refuse to acknowledge Yahweh
and his authority; but this is a false perspective. God's
people must not be deceived. Micah assures them that this
is God's world and he is in control even of history (4:8–13;
7:8–10).

2. *Judgment*

The book begins with a fearsome picture of God's anger
(1:2–5). In 6:1, 2 he brings formal charges, accusing the
people of sinning against him. 1:6–7 predict the destruction
of Samaria with all its religious trappings. This destruction
had taken place; but Judah had not learned from her
neighbour's mistakes. So 1:8–16 describe the advance of
an invading army into Judah. The future holds disaster
and calamity (2:3). Prayer will be useless (3:4). The agony
of Jerusalem will be as intense as that of a woman in
childbirth (4:10).

Micah took no pleasure in giving this message of doom.
He felt some hope for the distant future (7:7), but in the
present only great sorrow (7:1–6). He knew Judah deserved

what was coming to it. As we read 2:1–2, 8–9; 6:9–12 we glimpse a society where unscrupulous people are lying and cheating in order to take over farms and evict the occupants. The law courts and the religious centres were both controlled by greedy, self-seeking men (3:1–2). Self-interest and lack of trust had deformed all social relationships (7:2–6). The incredible thing was that all this was happening in a nation that was supposed to be united together in a covenant relationship with God (6:1–5). Tragically, here was one of the reasons for their plight: they counted on the fact that the God of the covenant was among them to keep them safe from trouble (3:11). Their sin was precisely that they had ignored the laws which were a basic part of the covenant.

The book reads as if Micah expected the final disaster to come in 701 BC when the Assyrians invaded. In fact, perhaps because of Hezekiah's reformation, Judah was miraculously delivered at that time (2 Kings 18–20). But the end had to come. Micah was right to recognize this as inevitable for a people who refused to acknowledge God. It came just over a century later after years of growing crises.

3. *Responsibility*

Micah had very definite ideas on what it meant to be a messenger from God, or to be a leader of God's people. Leaders were responsible before God for the well-being of the people, for speaking out God's truth even when nobody wanted to listen and for reflecting God's justice (3:8). But instead of caring for the people like shepherds, the leaders had behaved like butchers. 3:2–3 gives a terrible picture of the dehumanization that was taking place; the people, God's people, were being treated merely as meat to be abused and destroyed at the will of their leaders. Having so failed to meet the needs of the people, they were quite wrong to expect that God would continue to meet their needs (3:4). Professional prophets were betraying their calling just as much as government officials. The messages they gave depended not on any God-given insight but on the payment they received. Their punishment will again fit their crime. They will completely lose any genuine ability to prophesy and hence will end up with no job to do (3:5–7).

But the people themselves were not devoid of responsibility. They listened only to prophets who said what they wanted to hear, always looking for the easy answer. They did not realize that the kind of message that leaves one feeling happy does not always come from God, sometimes it is simply the result of 'plenty of wine and beer' (2:8–11)! They were responsible for testing the teaching they received. It was only to be accepted if it fitted in with what they knew of God, who was loving and forgiving, but also the holy, just and righteous sovereign Lord.

4. *The Glorious Future*

Micah's message of judgment was based on his knowledge of God. So was his hope for the future. The punishment would come, but it did not mean that God had forgotten them. Even before it happened he was planning to restore and save any who followed him (2:12 speaks of a remnant). These can look forward with confidence to the time when God will act. Jerusalem will be rebuilt and become the centre of a world at peace (4:1–3, 8; 7:11). The remnant will come back in triumph from exile (2:12–13; 4:6, 10; 5:7, 8). Hostile nations that may now appear to have the upper hand will be conquered (4:11–12; 5:8; 7:16–17). But those from all nations who acknowledge God will be able to have a real share in his kingdom (4:2–4).

In 5:2–5, in a very familiar passage often read at Christmas, we are told that one aspect of the hope for the future is that a Messiah will come. Israel and her rulers will be humiliated and abandoned (5:1, 3) but after that a ruler will come. He will be a real shepherd to God's people, truly acting on God's behalf and in God's way. He will be the one who will guarantee their peace.

TASTERS IN MICAH

Micah 2:1–5

Woe to those who plan iniquity,
  to those who plot evil on their beds!
At morning's light they carry it out
  because it is in their power to do it.
They covet fields and seize them,   2
  and houses, and take them.
They defraud a man of his home,
  a fellow-man of his inheritance.
Therefore, the LORD says: 3
  'I am planning disaster against this people,
  from which you cannot save yourselves.
You will no longer walk proudly,
  for it will be a time of calamity.
In that day men will ridicule you;   4
  they will taunt you with this mournful song:
"We are utterly ruined;
  my people's possession is divided up.
He takes it from me!
He assigns our fields to traitors."'
Therefore you will have no-one in the assembly   5
  of the LORD to divide the land by lot.

Micah's statements about God's anger at Israel do not come out of the blue. The reasons for the condemnation and destruction of Jerusalem are explicit.

Verse 1 pictures people lying awake at night scheming how they will cheat their fellows. Coveting, hankering after the property of somebody else, is itself strongly condemned in the law (Exodus 20:17; Deuteronomy 5:21). Here they not only covet but seize; oppressing the poor probably by both legal and illegal means. But God too is making plans; plans to punish them in an appropriate manner. The greedy and powerful men who seek to enlarge their estates at the expense of the inheritances of the poor — remembering that land was seen as a sacred trust to hand on to the next generation — will lose their own inheritances and will have no right (v5) to take part in any new redistribution of land.

Micah 6:6–8

With what shall I come before the LORD   6
    and bow down before the exalted God?
Shall I come before him with burnt offerings,
    with calves a year old?
Will the LORD be pleased with thousands of rams,   7
    with ten thousand rivers of oil?
Shall I offer my firstborn for my transgression,
    the fruit of my body for the sin of my soul?
He has showed you, O man, what is good.   8
And what does the LORD require of you?
To act justly and to love mercy
    and to walk humbly with your God.

These verses come in the context of a court case. Israel was charged with failing to keep the covenant. The opening speech has shown that Israel had no excuse for turning away from God because he had done so much for them. It is possible that verses 6–8 continue this speech by the prophet, as he asks a series of rhetorical questions with the presumed answer 'no', before he builds up to the climax of verse 8. But perhaps more likely is that this is the people's response to the appeal made by God in verses 3–5. They recognize that they do owe allegiance to God and are asking, somewhat petulantly perhaps, just what kind of gifts and service it is that God wants. They have already been bringing the normal sacrifices, so what is God quibbling about? Does he want improved quality, all the burnt offerings to be of the most expensive year old calves? Or is it quantity he is looking for, thousands of rams and rivers of oil? Or does he really want them to copy neighbouring states and bring human sacrifices; will that deal with their transgression?

Whether the prophet or the people are speaking in 6–7 the point is the same. Judah has wrongly assumed that slavishly keeping all the right rituals is what God wants of them. But in verse 8 they are reminded that God has already made quite clear what was involved in keeping the covenant, *ie* in doing what is 'good'. Micah is not giving a new answer, he is simply reminding them of the covenant law (Ex 20:1–17; Deut 10:12, etc.). God requires them to 'act justly', that is to apply the law properly and fairly and to ensure that there is no hint of oppression. They must 'love mercy', the word used for mercy here is sometimes translated as 'kindness' or 'steadfast love'. It is the deep loving covenant loyalty that God shows towards his people. In other words they are to behave towards one another as God behaves towards them. Also they must 'walk humbly with your God', which includes the proper ceremonial but also involves constant awareness of just where they stand in relation to God. What God is actually asking for then, is the total commitment of their whole lives; no lesser sacrifice will do.

MICAH FOR TODAY

What difference then does, or at least should, Micah's teaching make to our own lives? How far does his message, addressed to the kingdom of Judah in the eighth century BC, apply to Christians today? Like Amos and Hosea, Micah stresses that religion which is only a matter of appearance or only affects us on the surface is absolutely useless. That remains as true today as it was then. We must ask ourselves if there are areas of our lives that contradict our claim to be followers of Jesus. In particular, Micah keeps stressing the part that justice plays in this. As we read through the book it is obvious that for Micah justice is something very practical and down-to-earth. It is not just an abstract concept to support in theory but meaning very little in practice. Are there areas in my life where I am acting unjustly towards others, or where I know others are being unfairly treated and yet I do nothing about it? And does my concern for the needs of the underprivileged go beyond simply making sure that their legal requirements are strictly met.

For any who are involved in leadership Micah has a special message. Are we using this position simply to feather our own nest or (perhaps for most of us more of a problem) to bolster our own self-esteem? Do we honestly search for God's message and proclaim it fearlessly, or are we unduly influenced by telling people what they want to hear? Or, and perhaps again this is a more serious danger because more subtle, are we laying so much emphasis on one particular teaching, which may in itself be quite correct, that the whole picture becomes completely distorted. Do we for example, as Micah's contemporaries did, stress God's love and forgiveness to the exclusion of his anger at sin and disobedience?

Micah also teaches that all of us have the responsibility of making sure that what we are taught really fits in with what we already know from Scripture of God, and his requirements of love and of justice. Am I willing to listen when what I hear may make me uncomfortable and challenge me to action, or do I just go around looking for the message that makes me feel comfortable, and ignore everything else?

But Micah ends on a triumphant proclamation of God's forgiveness and of hope for the future. Have I really grasped the fact that God can take and transform any situation, however hopeless it may seem and even if it is caused by my own stupidity or deliberate disobedience? Because of Jesus we can have an even clearer hope and a greater certainty of this than Micah did. Does my awareness of the fact that Micah's promised ruler from Bethlehem has come, and that eventually God's kingdom will be fully instituted, influence my whole attitude to life? Do I really live in the light of that hope?

CHAPTER 9

Isaiah: the Man and the Book

ISAIAH THE MAN

Isaiah's involvement with king Hezekiah is mentioned in 2 Kings 19–20 and 2 Chronicles 32, but most of our knowledge about his life comes from the book of Isaiah and in particular chapters 7–8 and 36–39. He was the son of Amoz (not to be confused with the prophet Amos), and based in Jerusalem. He seems to have belonged to a wealthier and more socially influential family than any of the other eighth century prophets. Tradition suggests that he was himself a cousin of Uzziah and thus of royal blood. He was certainly well-educated, familiar with the king's court and a trusted advisor of Hezekiah. 2 Chronicles 26:22 may imply that he was a trained writer-historian employed as the royal recorder during the reign of Uzziah; if so, this could be one reason why he felt Uzziah's death so strongly. His own wife was a prophetess (8:3) (it is sometimes assumed that this was simply a courtesy title accorded to the wife of a prophet, but there are several prophetesses mentioned in the Old Testament and no evidence for the use of the term as 'Mrs Prophet'). They had two sons, Shear-Jashub and Maher-Shalal-Hash-Baz (7:3; 8:3). These names, which mean 'A remnant will return', and 'Swift to the spoil, speed the plunder' were used to emphasize Isaiah's message.

He was both an able politician and poet as well as being

a gifted prophet and teacher. In his writings we see him reflecting on ideas and historical events as well as recording direct messages to the people. Isaiah received an unmistakable call from God to be a prophet and to proclaim to unwilling listeners a message of judgment, exile and the eventual return from exile of a mere remnant of the nation (Isaiah 6). The vision which conveyed this call had a profound influence on Isaiah. This first-hand experience of God's greatness and holiness, the sense of his own sin and unworthiness, of receiving cleansing and forgiveness and of being commissioned to speak for God gave force to his message and strength and encouragement to Isaiah himself in what were really very difficult times. Echoes of this experience are found throughout his writings.

THE BOOK

The book of Isaiah is one of the longest in the Old Testament and one of the most important. It is significant because of its role in the history of Israel — as a warning in the time leading up to the exile, an encouragement and an inspiration during the exile and a challenge in post-exilic times. It is also important because of its very profound theological insight and teaching. The understanding of God presented in Isaiah is assumed and built on in the New Testament. It is so clear that in most cases the New Testament writers simply refer to Isaiah rather than repeating such teaching themselves. In fact, it is one of the most quoted Old Testament books within the New Testament. It would not be easy to understand the New Testament without some conception of Isaiah's teaching about God and his purposes for mankind. The prominent place accorded to the book in the Qumran library shows the importance it also had for the community associated with the Dead Sea Scrolls.

The book divides fairly clearly into four separate sections. Chapters 1–35 are prophecies addressed to the situation at the end of the eighth century BC. Chapters 36–39 is a historical narrative dealing with the reign of Hezekiah and Isaiah's part in certain incidents in Hezekiah's life. Chapters 40–55 are addressed to the Israelite community in exile and are written from the perspective of one who shares that exile and is also looking forward to its end. Chapters 56–66 seem to assume that the return to Jerusalem has already taken place and that the returned remnant is less committed to living as Yahweh's covenant people than had been hoped.

Within these sections it is not easy to trace a plan of design. The different passages do not seem to have been arranged according to either style or subject matter. We have a mixed assortment of judgment oracles, hope oracles, poems, illustrations, historical references and theological reflections.

Because these sections seem to be written from different perspectives and with different readers in mind, it is taken for granted by a large majority of scholars that the book contains the work of at least two, probably three and possibly more authors. Isaiah of Jerusalem is seen as responsible only for chapters 1–39. A prophet in the exile otherwise unknown and usually referred to as Deutero-Isaiah, or Second Isaiah, was responsible for chapters 40–55, and chapters 56–66 are assigned to a third writer, or collection of writers, known for convenience as Trito-Isaiah.

Amongst the factors that need to be taken into account in assessing the authorship and the unity of Isaiah are the following:

(a) 1–39 clearly deals with the time of Isaiah of Jerusalem. It includes many historical references. The section contains specific messages of judgment, but there is also penetrating theological reflection.

(b) 40–55 deals with the time of the exile and gives hope and encouragement for return. There are no historical references to Isaiah himself and there are very detailed references to Cyrus of Persia and to events which took place just before the return from exile. Unless one assumes, as some scholars do, that predictive prophecy is impossible, these phenomena do not in themselves preclude Isaiah's authorship. However Old Testament prophecy does not in general seem to be of the form which gives such detailed predictions nor does it normally announce in advance the names of those God has chosen to work for him.

(c) 56–66 is a message of salvation which presupposes the teaching of earlier chapters, but is apparently addressed to those who were living in the time after the first return from exile. These chapters are often felt not to express quite the same depth of theological insight that we find in 40–55.

(d) There is no evidence at all to show that any of the three parts ever existed separately. If separate authors were responsible for the latter half of the book then they must have written with the express intention of attaching their material to Isaiah's work. Because of this, some have suggested that there was a school of Isaiah's disciples, who continued to study his work and it was within this circle that the later chapters were written.

(e) There are many connections between the different sections, with parallel references, terminology and thought patterns. One only has to look down a list of cross references, such as may be found in a reference Bible, to see just how many links there are between the different sections of Isaiah.

(f) Notwithstanding these links there are significant differences of emphasis. It has been suggested that these can be accounted for by the differences in subject matter. But it is not altogether clear that the subject matter alone can explain the differences.

Whatever conclusion we come to about unity and authorship, two points must be kept in mind by anybody who studies Isaiah. Firstly, whether chapters 40–66 were written by Isaiah, or by other prophets used by God at the time in question, they are to be understood in an exilic and post-exilic setting. Secondly, whatever its origin, the book as we have it is a unity. The teaching of each section must be seen in the context of the others. In particular, it would be quite wrong to concentrate on the glorious picture of hope given in 40–55 without recognizing the sombre context of the judgment proclamations of 1–39.

It would be possible to summarize the message of Isaiah as a whole, but in view of the length of the book and the amount of teaching it contains, as well as because of the questions about authorship we will consider separately the three major sections.

CHAPTER 10

Isaiah 1–39

OUTLINE

THE MESSAGE

The teaching of Isaiah 1–39 is very closely related to the teaching of Micah. The message is largely one of judgment but there is also a very clear offer of hope for the remnant who repent; a hope that after the judgment life will be very different, It is as if Isaiah is trying to keep a fine balance. On the one hand he wants to ensure that those who really are following Yahweh and living as the covenant people should realize that God is sovereign and that his kingdom will eventually be established so that they need not get disheartened. But he is also determined to carry out his commission to proclaim judgment on a 'deaf nation'. They must not think that the hope for the future of the remnant in any way lessens the force or the reality of God's judgment on them.

The God of Judah

For Isaiah, as for all the prophets, teaching the people about God was of utmost importance. They could not relate to God or understand his dealings with them unless they knew what he was like. One of the most significant aspects of God's nature as far as Isaiah was concerned, was *holiness* (8:13). He characteristically describes God as 'the Holy One of Israel' (1:4; 5:19, 24; 10:20; 12:6; 17:7; 29:19; 30:11, 12, 15 etc. This title is used throughout the different sections of Isaiah, there are 12 occurrences in 1–39, 11 in 40–55, 2 in 56–66 and only 6 outside of this book). God's holiness is also clearly portrayed in Isaiah's vision (chapter 6). Because God was holy it was essential that his people reflect that holiness, and the remnant that will eventually be saved is described as the 'holy seed' (6:13) who will walk in the 'way of holiness' (35:8). The concept of holiness involves the idea of separateness, being set apart from the ordinary or everyday, and of purity. It is not restricted to moral 'goodness' but is closely linked with both glory and power. God's holiness is a 'terrible consuming splendour' (T. C. Vriezen *An Outline of Old Testament Theology* Blackwell 1970).

Isaiah also presents God as *sovereign and powerful*. He alone is to be exalted, no human being, however influential, no idol is anything in comparison with him (2:8–11, 17–21; 10:13). He is the one who created and controls the universe (37:16–18; 11:10–16; 14:24; 24:1–3). He is totally *just and righteous*, and deeply concerned for justice; he will certainly judge those who reject his law and who behave unjustly (30:18; 1:24–26; 3:13–15; 5:16). But he is also the God of *great compassion* who will act as saviour to all who repent (12:2; 14:1; 17:10; 30:18; 38:20). He is completely dependable and trustworthy (8:17; 10:20).

The Future for Judah

Isaiah refers constantly to the future time when God will take action about Judah. This 'day of the Lord' has two aspects. It will be a time of judgment and destruction but it will also be the time when God's kingdom of peace and justice will be instituted. This second aspect seems to present a deliberate ambiguity. There are clear historical references to Judah's being rescued from the invading Assyrians, subsequently conquered and destroyed by Babylon and then being redeemed from exile. But in addition the prophecies look beyond their own time to the time when the Messiah will come and to the end times when God's intervention in history will be dramatic and final. Later Old Testament passages, and also the New Testament, certainly interpret Isaiah's prophecies in both these ways.

1. Judgment and Destruction.
Isaiah makes it clear that God will judge Judah, but he shows with equal clarity that that judgment is not arbitrary or undeserved. He describes the ways in which the nation has rebelled against God and refused to conform to God's righteousness. Their lifestyle is corrupt (1:4) and their system of justice perverted (1:21–23; 5:23, 10:1–2) so they can be denounced as 'rulers of Sodom' and 'people of Gomorrah' (1:10). Their worship is totally unacceptable to God, 'Your incense is detestable to me. . . . I cannot bear your evil assemblies'. The reason is that their 'hands are full of blood' and they do not 'seek justice, encourage the oppressed or defend the cause of the fatherless' (1:11–17). They are oppressive: 'The plunder from the poor is in your houses. What do you mean by . . . grinding the faces of the poor?' (3:14–15). The rich women are more interested in fashion and status than in justice and kindness (3:16–17). Some rich people own several houses when others have become homeless (5:8); greed and drunkenness is a hallmark of their society (5:11, 22). As well as all these social crimes, they have turned to other nations rather than to God for guidance and support and they have freely allowed pagan idolatrous worship to take place (2:18; 10:11; 30:1–5).

   In view of God's holiness, as perceived by Isaiah, there is nothing surprising about the prediction that he was going to act in judgment against the people of Judah. The results of God's judgment are described in some detail. The prosperity of the nation would cease, even supplies of basic necessities like food and water would dry up, leadership of all kinds — military, judicial, administrative and economic would fail and the country would become destitute (3:1–26). Those who had oppressed others would themselves be oppressed; those who had unthinkingly built up great wealth would be impoverished; the nation which had been so proud would become an object of shame. Jerusalem, the city of David, was going to be destroyed and its inhabitants exiled. (5:8–38; 22:1–19; 29:1 – 30:17). The Assyrians, who would destroy the northern kingdom, would also bring devastation to Judah (8:1–8). However, Assyria would in fact be resisted and Judah delivered from its power (8:9–10). But this escape did not mean that Judah would be exempt from further judgment. Because they ignored the lessons of the Assyrian invasion, God would act again, using Babylon as his instrument and Jerusalem would this time be defeated and destroyed (39:5–7).

2. Salvation

Isaiah was told not to stop declaring judgment on Judah 'until the cities lie ruined and without inhabitant, . . . until the LORD has sent everyone far away and the land is utterly forsaken' (6: 11–12). However for those who were willing to listen he had also another message, of hope for a new life and a new kingdom of peace where God would reign in justice and righteousness. There would be 'survivors in Israel . . . who will be called holy' (4:2–3). Elsewhere they are described as 'a stump in the land' consisting of 'the holy seed' (6:13), and a 'remnant of Israel' who 'will truly rely on the LORD' (10:20). For this cleansed, renewed and repentant remnant, the future was something to await with joyful anticipation (30:18). A time will come when there will be no more gloom (9:1). The scattered people will be gathered together (11:12). Jerusalem will again be established as a centre of justice and people of all nations will come to see life being lived as God intended (2:2–4). The peace will be such as to affect not only other nations (2:4) but also the natural world (11:6–9).

As with the prophecies of judgment, so in these prophecies of blessing it is not always clear when Isaiah is referring to the historical situation and predicting a return from exile and when he is looking further forward to the 'last days'. In either case a recurrent theme is the saviour whom God would send to bring in his renewed kingdom. This Messiah (the word means anointed one, and reflects the practice of anointing with oil those who were appointed to special tasks) is described in different ways. He is the son specially given by God, and destined to 'reign on David's throne', honoured as the 'Wonderful Counsellor, Mighty God, Everlasting Father, Prince of Peace' (9:6–7). He is the shoot from the stump of Jesse, on whom the Spirit of the Lord will rest and who will rule with absolute justice and with a penetrating concern for the needs of the poor (11:1–5). He is the righteous king who will rule when God's spirit is poured out and the people again dwell in peace (32:1,15–18).

The Future for the Nations

Isaiah was aware that the sovereignty of God extended not simply over Israel and Judah but over all the nations. But for Isaiah, God's relationship with the nations was not simply one of power and control: he also had a loving concern for them. As with Israel and Judah, this concern expressed itself both in making clear that they were accountable to a righteous judge, and also in providing them too with the opportunity of salvation.

1. Judgment and Destruction

God had used nations such as Assyria to carry out his judgments against Israel and against Judah, but this did not mean that the nations were exempt from punishment. They would not be condemned, of course, for breaking the covenant, but they were judged and would be punished because of their cruel and oppressive behaviour, both within their own countries and towards other nations. In particular they are condemned for their treatment of God's people, even where that treatment may actually have furthered God's own purposes. More than a quarter of

Isaiah 1–39 is specifically concerned with prophecies about
other nations (chapters 13–21, 23–24, 34). He mentions
Babylon, Moab, Aram, Egypt, Arabia; there can be no
question about the extent of Yahweh's sovereignty.

In most of these chapters Isaiah is explaining to his
fellow countrymen that these nations will be punished for
their oppressive behaviour. Even the all-powerful Babylon
will be wiped out of existence (13:20). In chapter 24 we
even read that the whole earth is guilty — 'defiled by its
people' (v5), — and therefore the whole earth will come
under God's judgment. Paradoxically, the response to this
wholesale punishment both 'in the east' and 'from the
west' ought to be joy, because it proclaims the righteousness and justice of the Sovereign LORD (vv 14–16).

2. Salvation

The judgment on the nations is comprehensive, but judgment is not God's only message to them. In the glorious
future God has planned for his covenant people, there is
a place for those from other nations. In Isaiah 1–39 we
have the clearest vision in all the Old Testament of the
breadth with which the God of Israel reaches out to all
nations. Israel holds the key to the future, and Jerusalem
is the place where Isaiah envisages the new world-wide
kingdom of God coming together. There is never any hint
in the whole of the Bible of other nations finding their own
way to God by a route which bypasses the means of
salvation that God has provided through his people.
(Similarly, the New Testament makes it clear that forgiveness and relationship with God is only possible through
Christ.)

But this salvation, although it comes to and by means
of Israel, is by no means limited to them. It is for 'all the
nations'. The phrase occurs in Isaiah 2:2–4, a key passage
which is quoted in Micah 4:1–3. It portrays the ideal
relationship between the nations and Israel. A time will
come when they will share with Israel in the knowledge
of Yahweh, will be freely admitted to his house and even
receive the law. In 25:6 the nations are envisaged as taking

part in God's feast alongside his own people. These references can be interpreted as meaning that converts from all nations could become part of the nation of Israel, an idea which would not have been acceptable to some Israelites.

However in chapter 19 Isaiah goes even further than that. What he says is so remarkable that the passage is often assumed to be a later insertion into the text. The chapter describes God dealing with Egypt within Egypt and without any direct connection with the nation of Israel. V19 even predicts there will be an acceptable centre for the worship of Yahweh outside of Jerusalem. Vv20–22 clearly illustrate God's concern for the well-being of non-Israelite nations and his willingness to heal and restore them as well as to judge them. Verses 24–25 offer a challenging vision of Egypt and Assyria both standing alongside Israel as the people of God rather than as the subjects of Israel. Certainly it is Yahweh, the God of Israel, whom they come to acknowledge and worship, but they do so in their own right.

CHAPTER 11

Isaiah 40–66

ISAIAH 40–55

150 years separate the events being described in Isaiah 1–39 from the situation addressed in Isaiah 40–55. The first hundred years were marked in Judah by increasing corruption and growing political turmoil. This was interrupted by the reformation which took place in the reign of Josiah, but which, like Hezekiah's reforms apparently had no lasting effect on the people as a whole. The country came under Babylonian control, rebelled, and suffered defeat. A number of key people were taken into exile and a puppet king appointed. When he too rebelled, Jerusalem was besieged and eventually conquered and destroyed. All but the poorest people were exiled. So the community addressed in Isaiah 40–55 had been in exile in Babylon for more than fifty years.

These chapters recognize that the judgment so clearly prophesied in 1–39 has already happened. The focus now is on salvation and in particular deliverance from exile. They are written to encourage and to challenge the exiled community. Their great God was going to act — they must prepare to make the long journey home and be ready to serve God there, as he wants them to. What actually happened was that Babylon was defeated, by Cyrus of Persia who instituted a quite different policy in relation to

exiles which meant that they were not only permitted to
return to their homelands but encouraged to do so.

OUTLINE

THE MESSAGE

The view of God presented in these chapters probably
surpasses any other in the Old Testament. They offer such
profound teaching about God, his salvation and his servants
that it is impossible to do it justice without a detailed
treatment of virtually every verse. To appreciate these
chapters, it is essential to read them through at one sitting
and absorb the majesty and diversity of what they have
to say about God. However, this magnificent presentation
of what we might today describe as theology is by no
means unrelated to everyday life. Quite the reverse. The
teaching is presented in the context of a real pastoral
concern for the exiles and their needs. It displays a deep
understanding of their feelings and fears after so many
years of exile. They are disheartened and depressed, and
even those who have repented of the sins which led to the
exile may feel that Judah has sunk, as did the northern

kingdom, too low to be restored. They are tempted to
assume that the power of the Babylonians and their gods
is actually greater than the power of Yahweh, particularly
in Babylon itself. These chapters interact with and respond
to these fears by showing who God is and what he is about
to do. Once the people have grasped these truths, then all
their fears will be seen to be groundless.

Proclamation of God

The exiles need to realize the extent of God's power. He
is the 'Sovereign LORD' (40:10). As Creator he is sovereign
over the universe and the natural forces within it (40:21–26;
41:17–20; 42:5; 45:11–12, 18; 51:6). As the one who controls
creation he is no less sovereign over all human powers
and authorities. In comparison with Yahweh, the nations
are like 'a drop in a bucket' or 'dust on the scales' (40:15);
that is, they exist but are insignificant and may be safely
ignored in any transaction (41:1–2; 45:1; 52:10). Certainly
he is sovereign over the gods of other nations, those idols
who in reality are not only powerless but non-existent
(40:18–20; 41:21–24; 42:17; 44:6–23)! He is sovereign over
history, lord of the past and of the future (42:21 – 43:13).
History is directed by God in terms of his own plans and
purposes, so that both their present troubles and the
return from exile are not isolated meaningless events but
part of the total 'salvation history' of God's dealings with
his people and with other nations.

Anybody who grasps the truth of God's sovereignty is
led automatically to an acceptance of absolute monotheism.
The uniqueness of Yahweh, the One and Only True God,
is proclaimed in these chapters more clearly and more
explicitly than anywhere else in Scripture. God neither
seeks nor needs any help in planning or carrying out his
purposes. He is omniscient and omnipotent. He is the
Holy One; his sovereign lordship is so obvious that the
prophet cannot conceive how anyone could doubt it
(40:12–17; 43:1–13). But this sovereign, holy God is not

distant from his people. He is the Holy One *of Israel* who cares for them, is involved with them and acts on their behalf. Holiness is often linked with fear, but Israel are told 'Fear not' (41:10–14). The reason they need not fear, as the prophet is keen to point out, is that the Holy One is also their Redeemer (43:14; 44:6–24; 45:15). The God who created the world and sustains it, is the the one who created Israel and he will also sustain them, helping them in their troubles. The creative and the redemptive power of God go hand in hand. These emphases on absolute monotheism, the link between creation and eternity and the link between creation and redemption are often ident-ified as the most important distinctive insights in Deutero–Isaiah.

These chapters present God as the Mighty Warrior who will fight for his people, yet he is also the gentle shepherd who will care for them with infinite tenderness and love (40:9–11; 42:16; 43:2–4; 49:9–10). To grasp the truth of God's sovereignty while overlooking the extent of his mercy and the depth of his love would be to miss completely the point of Isaiah's proclamation. God has not only the power to deliver Israel; he also has the desire to do so. His majestic authority is matched by his tenderness and his sympathy. He is full of understanding and of gracious generosity and forgiveness. Israel belong to him and as he acted as their God in judgment he will now also do so in redemption. They are precious to him and he will pay whatever price is needed to set them free. He will take them up from their exile in Babylon and will lead them back, doubting and inadequate as they are, to the place where he wants them to be.

The Servant of Yahweh

Of great significance in these chapters is the 'Servant of Yahweh'. It is clear that God's activity in history is often mediated through human instruments. Isaiah 40–55 con-tains several references to 'servants' of God. Among these

are Israel, Cyrus the unbelieving Persian king who would
be responsible for allowing the exiles to return home, and
the prophet himself. There are also four passages, known
as the 'servant-poems' or 'servant-songs' which describe
the character and the task of the servant of Yahweh (42:1–
4; 49:1–6; 50:4–11; 52:13 – 53:12). The task of the servant is
to make God known and to be his instrument in bringing
justice to Israel and to the nations. He is specifically
equipped for this task by the Spirit of God. Various
suggestions have been made as to the identity of this
servant, the main one being nation of Israel; the faithful
remnant; the prophet himself; Cyrus; and the coming
Messiah. However, there is no reason to assume that
every reference is to the same servant, or that any reference
can be applied only to one figure.

In some places there seems to be a distinction between
the servant, who faithfully carries out the will of Yahweh,
and the nation Israel, who has failed in the task given to
her of reflecting Yahweh to the world (42:18–25; 49:4). It
is difficult to be precise and none of the suggested solutions
is without difficulties, but it is possible to trace a progression
from the picture of Israel as an unfaithful servant, to Cyrus
as an unknowing servant, to the prophet as a faithful and
willing servant, to what appears to be a more than human
messianic figure as the ideal servant.

The servant is first of all chosen by God (42:1). He is
gentle, caring, trustworthy, steadfast and committed to
establishing God's justice (42:2–4). He possesses deep
understanding and is a dedicated teacher (50:4), patient,
enduring and strong (50:6–7). His whole trust is in God
(50:9–10). His task involves great personal suffering, taking
on himself the sorrows and the punishment that really
belonged to others, in order that they may be healed (52:14
– 53:11). His work will be fruitful and he himself will
receive great honour (53:1, 12).

All the servant songs are seen by E. J. Young (*The Book
of Isaiah* vol 3, Eerdmans 1972) as primarily Messianic and
the New Testament certainly takes it for granted that these
passages can be applied to Christ (Mt 8:17; 20:28; Lk 2:32;

Jn 3:34; 12:38; Acts 8:32–35; Phil 2:7–9). The christological implications are very important — the New Testament makes it very clear that there is only one sin-bearer, only one who can take on himself the punishment deserved by others, only one who fits completely the ideal picture of the 'Servant of Yahweh' — but it would do the passages less than justice if we completely remove them from the context of the exiles in Babylon. God was working through particular 'servants' at that time, and in addition the people were being challenged to respond to God as his 'servants' should.

The Salvation

The salvation envisaged is first of all salvation from exile. For this reason it is appropriate to describe God as Redeemer (10 times in Isaiah 40–55, 3 times in Isaiah 56–66 and 4 times only in the rest of the Old Testament). This salvation will be achieved by means of a liberator from the East (41:2, almost certainly referring to Cyrus of Persia) but the controlling factor is quite clearly God himself. The language used deliberately calls to mind the Exodus from Egypt, though this new redemption is seen as even more significant. Combined with this redemption which is seen as taking place within history, there is also the idea of final redemption in the end times (sometimes described as eschatological redemption). The exiles are experiencing the beginning of the end. It is apparently implied that as they return they can in some way begin to appreciate and enter into the salvation that would be theirs when God intervened in history at the very end of time.

Sometimes redemption is seen outwardly, in terms of legal freedom from the control of enemies (41:13ff; 43:3, 14), but at other times also inwardly in a spiritual sense (40:28–31; 43:25; 44:22). The return is a return to God as well as a return to Jerusalem and thus offers forgiveness of sins as well as renewed material prosperity. Those who accept the challenge and choose to return will travel in

triumph to Israel; the new community to be established
will be peaceful, righteous and the ideal place to live
(41:12, 18–20; 42:6; 43:5, 19–21; 44:26–28; 49:8–26). Not
only will it be a pattern for other nations, it will also be
open for those from other nations who choose to join it.

This positive attitude to nations other than Israel, which
offers them the opportunity of salvation as well as proclaiming judgment on them for their failure to meet God's
demands, is one of the strongest links between 1–39 and
40–55. However, it should be noted that 40–55 never
displays the breadth of Isaiah 19; although in these chapters all the nations assemble at Jerusalem to worship the
one true God (45:14, 22; 49:14–25; 51:5; 55:5), it is Israel
which dominates the rest. Because they come to serve the
God of Israel, the nations are pictured as serving Israel
also. What is new in 40–55 is the missionary vision. Israel
is presented as having a positive responsibility to take the
message of Yahweh to the nations so that they can share
in the salvation of Israel. One of the highest purposes of
the election of Israel is that she should bring light to the
nations (42:1–7; 45:20–25; 49:1–6). It appears that this idea
was not immediately acceptable to the exiles and it is
suggested that Isaiah's disappointment with their response
led to a change in his presentation of the 'Servant of
Yahweh', focusing down from the nation as a whole to
concentrate on a single messianic individual. The people
were glad to hear the message of the righteousness of God
in so far as it entailed the punishment of the Gentiles, but
unwilling to accept that it could lead to their possible
inclusion in the new kingdom.

The prophecies of the return present a picture of glorious
triumph. Sadly, this was not matched by what actually
happened. One reason was the defective response of
those who returned; they fell short both in their faith and
obedience and as we have seen, all prophecy is to some
extent conditional on the response of those concerned.
Another factor to take into account is that some of the
language is poetic overstatement and not meant to be
taken literally. All the same, the words of Isaiah 40–55

describe a miracle which does not seem to be fully reflected in the reality. It is important not to underestimate how remarkable was the re-establishment of the Jerusalem community. Psalm 126 shows even the nations acknowledging that Yahweh has done 'great things' for his people. But the sense of incompleteness remains. The eschatological elements within the prophecy make it likely that the prophet recognized he was speaking both of the immediate historical situation and of times still to come. It is significant that John the Baptist refers 40:3 to himself and that Jesus quotes from these chapters. The New Testament writers were convinced that though the short-term fulfilment of these prophecies may have seemed incomplete, they have complete fulfilment in Jesus Christ.

ISAIAH 56–66

Scholars do not agree whether this part of Isaiah is a single unit or whether it is a compilation from several different sources. However, there is a unity of thought and theme within the chapters themselves and there can be no doubt that they were written in the context of a clear understanding of the earlier chapters of Isaiah. The setting appears to be the period after the first return from exile but before the re-organization and development programme set up by Ezra and Nehemiah, and probably also before the prophesying of Haggai and Zechariah which led to the completion of the temple rebuilding, that is, the time between 537 and 520 BC.

When in 538 BC Cyrus of Persia issued his decree that all those who had been compulsorily exiled should be allowed to return home, many Jews were so comfortably settled in Babylon that they declined to take up his offer. However, a small group of visionaries, inspired by the teaching of Isaiah 40–55 and by Ezekiel, seized the opportunity to go back. Led first by Sheshbazzar and later by Zerubbabel they began by building an altar and starting work on the temple. However it was a disappointing

experience. The land had been uncultivated in the inter-
vening years, there was fierce opposition from the local
population, they were disheartened by the hard work
involved and their enthusiasm collapsed. It is into this
situation of disillusionment and lost vision that these
chapters speak.

OUTLINE

THE MESSAGE

Isaiah 40–55 had envisaged the return from exile as a
tremendous turning point in the history of Israel and
indeed of the world, a time when God would reveal
himself in an unmistakable way and bring triumph and
glory to Israel. But the reality of the situation appeared to
be very different. A group had indeed returned from exile
but the brave new world they had expected seemed little
better than the world Israel had known before the exile.
There were similar difficulties, similar opposition and no
less faithlessness and disobedience among God's people.
Isaiah 56–66 is very realistic about all this (56:9–12; 57:6–
10; 59:3–15 etc.).

But these chapters also make clear that the same God
still controls the world and pronounces the same sentence

of judgment upon the unrighteous. There is still salvation for the righteous. This means that the same hope for the future that inspired the exiles in Babylon is relevant in Judah also, though it maybe has to be understood in a rather different way from their initial expectations. Here we can see how the great truths presented in the earlier chapters may still be understood as true even when some of the prophecies they contain appear to be unfulfilled.

Thus the central section of these prophecies, around which the rest are arranged is the clear proclamation of salvation found in chapters 60–62. Here we learn of the glory that will come to the community of God's people, centred on Zion. The chapters before and after these emphasize the responsibility of the people to live faithful and holy lives. This has in no sense been lessened by the exile or by the return from exile. God will still judge those of his people who turn away from him. God's action in regard to his people is still related to their own attitude and behaviour. But it is apparent that in Isaiah 56–66 the central proclamation remains that of the salvation that God will bring and the glorious hope that should sustain those who live righteous and faithful lives.

We have seen that in Isaiah 40–55 hope (in historical terms) is centred on the return from exile. In 56–66 it is focused rather on a transformation of the nation's present condition, though it also includes the full return of those members of God's people who are scattered throughout the lands. (This scattered population is often referred to as the *diaspora* or Dispersion.) It is worth noting that although 65:1–7 echoes the attitude of the eighth century prophets to sacrifice, nevertheless there is an assumption that in the new age both temple worship and sacrifice will take place (60:7; 62:9). In general these chapters portray salvation in materialistic historical terms, but there are also hints of an eschatological understanding. The full extent of God's glory will be realized only in the end times, with the coming of the new heavens and the new earth (66:17–25; 59:19–20).

Quite clearly in these chapters it is the nation of Israel

which is destined to receive the promise of salvation. However, this does not mean automatic destruction for the rest of the nations but rather the possibility of some form of inclusion in the restored state. The universalist teaching found in some of the earlier chapters in Isaiah (both 1–39 and 40–55) is less emphatic here and the nations are generally presented as servants of Israel, but parallels with the earlier chapters are easier to find than contradictions.

CHAPTER 12

Isaiah: Tasters and Application

TASTERS IN ISAIAH

6:5–10

'Woe to me!' I cried. 'I am ruined! For I am a man   5
   of unclean lips, and I live among a people of unclean
   lips, and my eyes have seen the King, the LORD
   Almighty.'
Then one of the seraphs flew to me with a live coal   6
   in his hand, which he had taken with tongs from the
   altar.
With it he touched my mouth and said, 'See, this   7
   has touched your lips; your guilt is taken away and
   your sin atoned for.'
Then I heard the voice of the LORD saying, 'Whom   8
   shall I send? And who will go for us?'
And I said, 'Here I am. Send me!'
He said, 'Go and tell this people: 9
   "Be ever hearing, but never understanding;
   be ever seeing, but never perceiving."
Make the heart of this people calloused;   10
   make their ears dull
   and close their eyes.
Otherwise they might see with their eyes,
   hear with their ears,
   understand with their hearts,
   and turn and be healed.'

These verses are possibly among the best known in Isaiah. In them the prophet describes the dramatic experience when he became aware of the call of God on his life and the message that God had given him to deliver. This experience had a very powerful effect on the whole of his ministry. In verses 1–4 we read of Isaiah's initial encounter with God which so impressed him with God's sovereignty and holiness that he could never be the same person again. Verse 5 shows how this vision of God resulted in a profound awareness of his own sinfulness and the sinfulness of his people. Although well aware of how far the Israelites had sunk, Isaiah made no attempt to separate himself from them, but rather he identified himself with them. This realization of the extent and seriousness of the nation's sin against God gave great force to Isaiah's proclamation of God's judgment.

Verses 6–7 recall Isaiah's personal experience of God's forgiveness, an experience which enabled him to envisage the possibility of forgiveness also being available for the sinful nation, so that he was able to announce hope even within his prophecy of judgment.

Verses 8–9a describe the call itself, though strictly speaking we have not a call, but the presentation of a task for which Isaiah subsequently volunteers. It is perhaps because of this that there is no sign of the kind of objecting to the given assignment that we see in other call narratives (Exodus 4:1–13; Jeremiah 1:6).

Verses 9b–10 contain the message that Isaiah is to proclaim. It takes account of the hardheartedness of the people. This hardheartedness means that they will not listen to Isaiah and therefore will not obey his call to 'turn and be healed'. The final section of this passage emphasizes that Isaiah's difficult task must continue until Judah is destroyed by divine judgment. The people will be decimated and only a 'stump' will remain (v 13). But the existence of that stump provides Isaiah with a reason for offering hope to those few Judeans who are true followers of Yahweh.

40:27–31

Why do you say, O Jacob,   27
  and complain, O Israel,
'My way is hidden from the LORD;
  my cause is disregarded by my God'?
Do you not know?   28
Have you not heard?
The LORD is the everlasting God,
  the Creator of the ends of the earth.
He will not grow tired or weary,
  and his understanding no-one can fathom.
He gives strength to the weary   29
  and increases the power of the weak.
Even youths grow tired and weary,   30
  and young men stumble and fall;
but those who hope in the LORD   31
  will renew their strength.
They will soar on wings like eagles;
  they will run and not grow weary.
  they will walk and not be faint.

This little section introduces many of the themes that are
taken up and developed in the following chapters. Firstly
it describes the present feelings of the exiles; then it
corrects their false impression of God; and finally it looks
to the future when their present situation will be totally
transformed.

In their dejected state the exiles had lost all confidence
in themselves and in their God. Isaiah quotes what must
have been a regular complaint among them. 'If Yahweh is
our God then he clearly doesn't realize what is happening
to us and if he knows he doesn't care'. The prophet is
incredulous. Had they really understood so little about
God that they could even begin to perceive him either as
not understanding or not caring? Yahweh is the everlasting Creator, there is nothing on earth that he does not
understand completely, though there were many things

about his knowledge and his actions that human beings were incapable of comprehending. Far from not caring, this God, in all his transcendence and power, has a particular concern for the weary and the weak. The prophet recognizes that weariness and weakness are part of the human condition, but they are never the last word for those who 'hope in Yahweh'.

This is no theoretical or abstract discussion. The situation of the exile is never far from the prophet's mind. The sovereign LORD is at work and invites Israel to co-operate with him by returning to their homeland. As they do this Yahweh will accompany them and bless them with his presence. It will be a long walk; they may start off running but in time they will be reduced to walking and ultimately exhaustion might be expected to overtake even fit young men — but their strength will be renewed and they will not faint.

55:6–13

Seek the LORD while he may be found;   6
    call on him while he is near.
Let the wicked forsake his way   7
    and the evil man his thoughts.
Let him turn to the LORD, and he will have mercy
    on him, and to our God, for he will freely pardon.
'For my thoughts are not your thoughts,   8
    neither are your ways my ways,' declares the
    LORD.
'As the heavens are higher than the earth,   9
    so are my ways higher than your ways,
    and my thoughts than your thoughts.
As the rain and the snow come down from heaven,   10
    and do not return to it without watering the earth
    and making it bud and flourish,
      so that it yields seed for the sower and bread for
      the eater,
so is my word that goes out from my mouth: 11

It will not return to me empty,
but will accomplish what I desire
and achieve the purpose for which I sent it.
You will go out in joy and be led forth in peace; 12
the mountains and hills will burst into song
before you,
and all the trees of the field will clap their hands.
Instead of the thornbush will grow the pine tree, 13
and instead of briers the myrtle will grow.
This will be for the LORD's renown,
for an everlasting sign, which will not be destroyed.'

As chapter 40 introduced the range of the prophet's concerns, so chapter 55 reiterates them. Here is a final invitation to the people to unite in responding to God's call and join and have a share in his great covenant kingdom. Verses 6–7 suggest that this opportunity may not always be available and make it clear that individuals do have a part to play if they are to receive salvation. Receiving mercy and forgiveness depend on turning to the LORD. But for all who do turn to him that pardon is freely available.

Verses 9–11 look back to 40:8, providing another reminder of God's wisdom and majesty and also of the permanence and effectiveness of his word. God's plans will be accomplished, his purposes will be carried out. The section closes with a reminder that part of these purposes is that the triumphant and joyful 'exodus' of the returning people, will be an eternal witness to the glory of God.

60:1–3

Arise, shine, for your light has come.
and the glory of the LORD rises upon you.
See, darkness covers the earth 2
and thick darkness is over the peoples,
but the LORD rises upon you
and his glory appears over you.

Nations will come to your light,   3
   and kings to the brightness of your dawn.

Jerusalem, as representative of the restored nation of Israel, is challenged to raise herself from the dark depression that is blighting her life. The return has not met the exiles' expectations. But they should look to the future where Israel will be given a light which will not only bring a fresh awareness of God, but will cause all nations to leave the surrounding darkness and join them. Israel is told to 'shine', that is, to have a shining face, to be joyful. This concept of light in the middle of darkness is paralleled in the plague narrative (Exodus 10:23) and also in Isaiah 9:2, and the general concept of Israel as a light comes in Isaiah 40:5; 42:6; 49:6, 7, etc. E. J. Young interprets the nations coming to the light as coming into a saving knowledge of the truth but it appears from vv 4–14 that in this case the nations come not so much to learn of Yahweh (as in Isaiah 2:2–4) but rather to bring tribute and to serve Zion.

The theme of this passage is not so much universalism or the inclusion of the nations, but rather the glorification of Zion. Zion, not the nations, is the focus of attention here; though perhaps a distinction ought to be made between the nations in general and those who as in chapter 55 have 'bound themselves to the LORD' (56:3). The clear message is that the defeat and disillusion of the first few years after the return is by no means the end of the story. Zion's finest hour is yet to come!

ISAIAH FOR TODAY

The number of quotations from Isaiah in the New Testament shows how important the message of Isaiah is for Christians. However, because Isaiah contains so many inspiring proclamations of hope for the future in the light of the greatness of God, Christians are liable to study and respond to these proclamations without taking note of their context. But to do that is to miss the point of the book as a whole which clearly sets the proclamation of a glorious future hope in the context of judgment and in the reality of a historical setting. The prophecies were addressed to Israel in a particular historical situation, and whereas the New Testament applies much of the teaching to the church as God's people in a different situation, it is important to look first of all at the context and understand the original meaning.

Having taken note of that warning, it would still be impossible in the space we have available to do justice to all that Christians can learn from Isaiah and we will have to be content with just a few pointers.

There is clear teaching in Isaiah (and also in the rest of Scripture), that it is only by learning more of God and his character that people can understand what life is about and know what are the right attitudes and the right behaviour in any situation. This is one reason why Isaiah's unsurpassed proclamation of God remains so important. Isaiah calls on his readers to worship and serve the God who is Creator and Redeemer, as Comforter and Judge, as the one who expects his people to act in a way that will forward his purposes, but who will if necessary act himself to ensure that his will is carried out (59:16). So can we assume that the only important thing is to understand the character of God and that to do this will lead to an easy life? Reading Isaiah 40–55 after 1–39 could leave that impression, but the addition of 56–66 shows that this is not the whole story.

Isaiah as a whole is full of creative tension. On the one hand he is an extremist, proclaiming absolutes which are uncompromising and possibly unacceptable both to the Jews of the time and to people today. There is only one God and he is the Sovereign Creator Lord, Yahweh of Israel. No other god can be compared with him or indeed has any real existence. No alternative perspective can be tolerated. This great God will judge and punish sinners even to the extent of allowing his own people to be decimated and exiled. The New Testament picks up this extremism when it asserts that there is no alternative route to God, salvation can only be found through Jesus Christ (John 14:6; Acts 4:12) and all those who reject this salvation will die (Romans 6:23; Galatians 6:7–8; Hebrews 2:1–3). On the other hand Isaiah expresses a flexibility that dogmatists might reject as leading to unacceptable compromise. For example, a pagan king is described as God's servant and those from other nations as having a full part in God's kingdom. Once more he might be criticized both by Jews of his own time and by our own contemporaries.

The tensions in Isaiah result in part from the constantly changing perspective. Sometimes his vision is directed to the past, sometimes to the present, sometimes to the future. Sometimes the account zooms in and focuses on a particular situation or incident; on other occasions it uses, as it were, a wide-angle lens and covers a broad spectrum of time and space. We see, on the one hand, a constant narrowing down of the concept of salvation so that the vast majority of the people of Israel and Judah are rejected and only a remnant remain. On the other hand we have a real opening up, so that salvation is not restricted to Israel but pictured as universal. What makes it possible for the tension to be maintained is the overwhelming conviction that although it is impossible for human beings, even righteous followers of God, to grasp, God has the whole display not only in his sights but under his control, and he can be trusted.

To accept the challenge of Isaiah is not easy. To maintain creative tension is always difficult. In this case it means that knowing and understanding God's sovereignty may demand from us an apparent extremism which proclaims absolute truths in a manner which may sound uncompromising and intolerant. Equally, awareness of God's greatness involves recognizing that we cannot see the whole picture at once, and that God may be acting and speaking in a way that is very different from our initial expectation. This calls for a humble flexibility which may appear to be compromising and wishy-washy.

The book makes it clear that living a life based on a knowledge of God and his character is not necessarily easy or comfortable. But, as each section of the book demonstrates it is infinitely worthwhile.

Isaiah contains many other thought-provoking insights. He affirms the reality of judgment, enriches our understanding of righteousness and holiness, emphasizes that divine action does not mean the end of our responsibility and portrays what it means to be a servant of God. These are important topics but they are often dealt with by the other prophets and we shall look at them in other contexts.

Questions for study and discussion

1. The messages of the eighth century prophets stem directly from the circumstances and behaviour of their own contemporaries. Can they therefore be seen as having any permanent relevance?

2. Outline the conditions in Israel and Judah at the time of the eighth century prophets and discuss which aspect of those conditions most dominated the thought of each prophet.

3. Compare and contrast the ministries of Amos and Hosea.

4. Discuss the way in which Amos's understanding of the character of God influenced his prophecies.

5. 'The message of Amos is directed to society rather than to individuals'. Discuss.

6. How far can the book of Amos be seen as a proclamation of human rights?

7. Analyse Amos's teaching about God's attitude to nations other than Israel.

8. Is it true to say Amos was more interested in social issues than in religious ones?

9. Are there any aspects of our own society (or of our own church), which would be likely to horrify a modern-day Amos? What would be appropriate ways to register such horror today?

10. Discuss the teaching in Amos on the relationship between religion and lifestyle. Think about this relationship in your own life.

11. 'Hosea's ministry was simply an extension of his life'. Discuss.

12. Is Hosea more properly described as a prophet of God's love or as a prophet of God's judgment?

13. To what extent are Hosea's writings dominated by the idea of the covenant?

14. What does Hosea teach about the terms God lays down for Israel's relationship with him?

15. Examine the imagery Hosea uses to describe the relationship between God and Israel. Suggest alternative pictures which could be used in today's world to get across the depth of feeling conveyed by Hosea.

16. Are there any ways in which Christians today could be accused of spiritual adultery? In such cases, what would be involved in restoring relationship with God?

17. Discuss Micah's teaching on the relative responsibilities of the leaders of God's people and the people themselves.

18. How does Micah relate the concept of justice both to God's holiness and to God's love?

19. How did Micah envisage the future for Judah?

20. What relevance could the book of Micah have in a discussion of modern Christian business ethics?

21. How valid is Micah's assessment that most corruption in a country is likely to stem from its capital city?

22. Consider the application of Micah 6:8 for the modern church and for our own lives.

23. In what ways was Isaiah's ministry influenced by his call?

24. Discuss the composition of the book of Isaiah bringing out the differences and the unifying factors between the different sections.

25. Explain the concept of holiness as it is portrayed in Isaiah 1–39.

26. How far is the presentation of the character of God in Isaiah 40–55 directly relevant to the circumstances of the Hebrews in exile?

27. Describe and evaluate the proclamation of absolute monotheism in Isaiah 40–55.

28. Consider the messianic and non-messianic implications of the 'Servant Songs'.

29. What difference do Isaiah 40–55 and Isaiah 56–66 see the exile as making in God's long-term plans for Israel?

30. Discuss the way in which Isaiah 56–66 tackles the apparent lack of fulfilment of earlier prophecies.

31. In the different sections of Isaiah, was it the prophet's own experience of relationship with God that gave him such insight into God's character, or his awareness of God's character that enabled him to experience such a close relationship with God?

32. Think about how far your own experience of God relates to your understanding of God's character, and vice-versa.

33. Consider areas in your own life or in the life of your church where the tension Isaiah presents between flexibility of ideas and uncompromising absolutes has not been maintained.

SUGGESTED FURTHER READING

Auld, A. G. *Amos* JSOT Press 1986

Hubbard, D. A. *Joel and Amos* (Tyndale) IVP 1989

Mays, J. L. *Amos* (Old Testament Library) SCM 1969

McKeating, H. *The Books of Amos, Hosea and Micah* (Cambridge Bible Commentary) CUP 1971

Motyer, J. A. *The Day of the Lion* IVP 1974

Soggin, J. A. *The Prophet Amos* SCM 1987

Stuart, D. *Hosea — Jonah* Word Biblical Commentaries 1987

Wolff, H. W. *Joel and Amos* (Hermeneia) Fortress Press 1977

Anderson, F. I. and D. N. Freedman *Hosea* (Anchor Bible) Doubleday 1980

Hubbard, D. A. *Hosea* (Tyndale) IVP 1989

Mays, J. L. *Hosea* (Old Testament Library) SCM 1969

Ward, J. M. *Hosea* Harper and Row 1966

Wolff, H. W. *Hosea* (Hermeneia) Fortress Press 1974

Allen, L. C. *The Books of Joel, Obadiah, Jonah and Micah* (NICOT) Eerdmans 1976

Baker, D. W. T. D. Alexander and B. K. Waltke *Obadiah, Jonah and Micah* (Tyndale) IVP 1988

Hillers D. R. *Micah* (Hermeneia) Fortress Press 1984

Mays, J. L. *Micah* (Old Testament Library) SCM 1976

Smith, R. L. *Micah — Malachi* Word Biblical Commentaries 1984

Clements, R. E. *Isaiah 1–39* (New Century Bible) MM&S 1980

Oswalt, J. N. *Isaiah 1–39* (NICOT) Eerdmans 1986

Watts, J. D. W. *Isaiah 1–33* Word 1985
——*Isaiah 34–66* Word 1987
Westermann, C. *Isaiah 40–66* (Old Testament Library) SCM 1969
Whybray, R. N. *The Second Isaiah* JSOT Press 1983
Young, E. J. *The Book of Isaiah* (3 volumes) Eerdmans 1965, 1969, 1972

SECTION III — UP TO THE EXILE

CHAPTER 13

Background: Up to the Exile

THE WORLD SITUATION

Assyria, which was the major power at the end of the eighth century, remained strong throughout the first half of the seventh century and although there were a few previous indications of problems ahead, it was not until the death of Ashurbanipal in 626 BC that things really began to go wrong for them. The influence of the Babylonians, in alliance with the Medes, was growing all the time and from 616 BC there was a full state of war between the two powers. In 612 BC the Assyrian capital, Nineveh, fell to the Babylonians and that really spelt the end of Assyrian power. In 609 BC the Egyptians, responding to the new threat from Babylon, began a campaign to support the Assyrians against the Babylonians. Josiah of Judah, perhaps fearing a resurgence of Assyrian power and influence, tried to intercept the Egyptian advance. He was killed in battle and Judah came under Egyptian overlordship. In 605 BC Babylon defeated Egypt at Carchemish in a way that established Babylonian supremacy over the whole region. It was at this time that Judah came under Babylonian control.

WITHIN JUDAH

After the fall of Samaria and the end of the northern

kingdom in 722 BC, adherents of Yahweh may have hoped that Judah would have learned from Israel's mistakes and followed a different path. Instead, as Isaiah and Micah had foreseen, the reforms which Hezekiah had initiated had no lasting effect. According to 2 Kings 21, Hezekiah's son, Manasseh, far from resisting Assyrian influences in Judah, welcomed them with open arms. The Assyrian Baalism, worship of Asherah, the mother goddess, and the star cults were encouraged; official shrines were even set up for foreign cults. Under Manasseh, all that was rotten in Judean society came once more to the surface. Idolatry, immorality and oppression were rampant. Opponents, presumably including those who remained faithful to Yahweh the God of Israel, were ruthlessly crushed. It is perhaps not surprising that although there were prophets who spoke out (2 Kings 21:10), no major writing prophet emerged during that time.

After reigning for approximately 45 years, Manasseh was succeeded by his son Amon who continued his father's policies but was assassinated after only two years. His son Josiah reigned from 640–609 BC. Josiah was only eight when Amon was killed and could not have been more different from his father or his grandfather. As he grew, so did his dedication to Yahweh. He instituted all sorts of political and religious reforms, throwing off Assyrian influence, and seeking to establish Judah as a nation living under God's covenant. However, after Josiah's death it became clear that his reforms had not touched the heart of the nation. The underlying corruption remained and the last four kings of Judah, Jehoahaz, Jehoiakim, Jehoiachin and Zedekiah are all described as evil.

Judah rebelled against Babylon several times between 609 and 587 BC. The result was first of all that a number of leaders and skilled workers were taken into exile. When there was further rebellion Babylon took decisive action. In 587 BC Jerusalem was besieged and destroyed, the Temple was looted, and a large proportion of the population was forced to join their fellow countrymen in exile.

THE PROPHETS

There were four major prophets who began their ministry during the second half of the seventh century. The underlying theology and approach of all of these, their attitude to God and to judgment and salvation is very similar, but their individual perspectives are rather different. Nahum looks at the terrible cruelty and oppression of Assyria and prophesies that judgment will certainly come to them. Zephaniah speaks of the judgment that was coming to Judah as well as to the rest of the world, but also of the salvation that would be available to the faithful remnant. Habakkuk writes as a man who believes in the righteousness and sovereignty of Yahweh and is baffled by the injustice and oppression he sees both within his own nation and outside. Jeremiah's much longer book addresses many different concerns. But above all he supplies a historical perspective, encouraging Judah to accept the exile as inescapable. It was inevitable because of their own sin and rebellion against God, but there was hope. God had not finished with Judah; there would be a return from exile and the possibility of a new relationship with God.

Nahum

OUTLINE

HISTORICAL AND LITERARY CONSIDERATIONS

This book is described as an oracle, (literally here a 'burden'), about Nineveh; the one who presents or carries this burden is Nahum the Elkoshite.

Outside of his book there is no mention of this or indeed any other Nahum in the Old Testament; although the name does occur in the genealogical list in Luke 3:25. We have no idea where Elkosh was situated, although certain traditions, which are impossible to substantiate, suggest that it might have been a village in Iran, or in Galilee. (It is just possible that the name Capernaum, meaning 'village of Nahum' is related to that tradition.) However, Nahum himself was almost certainly Judean and the most common suggestion is that he came from Beth-gabre, about twenty miles from Jerusalem and not too far from Micah's home town.

The prophecy dates some time after the Assyrian attack on Thebes in 663 BC (No-Amon, in some versions of Nahum 3:8, refers to Thebes) and before the fall of Nineveh in 612 BC. Whether we date the prophecy early or late within that time scale depends on whether Nahum's conviction that Nineveh would fall was based on a spiritual awareness of their corruption and its consequences, or whether, by the time he wrote, their end was also obvious politically. The impression of the book is that Assyria was still powerful, which would indicate a date before the death of Ashurbanipal in 626 BC. This means that Nahum wrote either in the later years of Manasseh or at the beginning of Josiah's reign.

The first verse indicates that unlike much of the prophetic material, Nahum originated in written rather than spoken form. The book does not divide easily into distinct sections, although in the three chapters the writer approaches his theme from different angles. The similarity of style throughout the book supports the view that the whole is the work of one prophet. There is debate as to whether chapter 1 includes an acrostic poem either written or quoted by Nahum. Certainly some kind of structure is present in the chapter, and several verses beginning with consecutive letters of the Hebrew alphabet, but several letters are missing and a great deal of conjectural emendation would be needed to restore some supposed 'original' form.

It has been suggested that Nahum was a Jerusalem cult prophet and the book was written as a cultic liturgy celebrating the destruction of Nineveh. The prophecy would certainly be appropriate as part of a national festival, but there is no evidence to show that it was actually written for that purpose and the book displays no special interest in Jerusalem. Neither Nineveh nor Assyria in general is mentioned until 2:8 but there is no dispute about the identity of the 'you' addressed in various places. For the sake of clarity, NIV has added 'O Nineveh' and 'O Judah' to the text in 1:11, 12 etc..

THE MESSAGE OF NAHUM

Nahum's name means 'comforter', but his message contains little comfort, particularly for Nineveh. He shows no sympathy for the Assyrians; they are an evil oppressive people, they deserve punishment and God will bring that punishment upon them. There is pathos, but no real regret in Nahum's recognition that no outsider will mourn Assyria's ruin (3:7). The fact is that everyone will rejoice about it (3:19).

Chapter 1 puts this message or 'burden' of destruction in the context of the character of God. Nahum has been described as a 'one-theme' prophet, but the proclamation of the destruction of Nineveh is not his main theme but rather an illustration of it. Nahum's central theme is the sovereignty of God. Yahweh, the mighty Lord of creation (1:4–6) is a 'jealous and avenging God' (1:2) who 'will not leave the guilty unpunished' (1:3). The ruin of Nineveh will make God's sovereignty clear and will show to Judah that God does care for those who trust in him (1:7) and does punish evil. The general picture of doom in Chapter 2 shows that the city of Nineveh will be totally destroyed, although it is not a detailed description of what is going to happen. Chapter 3 supplies further details of this destruction and further reasons why the 'city of blood' (3:1) so richly deserved her fate.

Nahum is one of very few prophets (Obadiah is another), who makes no mention of the sins of Judah. Considering the extent of the corruption in Judah during the reign of Manasseh (2 Kings 21), it is perhaps not surprising that some have even suggested that Nahum was a false prophet. Jeremiah condemned very strongly those who prophesied deliverance for Judah without making it clear that her own sins would have to be dealt with (Jeremiah 23). However, this fails to take into account Nahum's single theme of God's sovereignty and single illustration of Nineveh's ruin. The fact that God will punish evil is clear and Nahum contains no suggestion that Judah is exempt.

It may be relevant to note that in the Hebrew Bible the

twelve minor prophets formed one single book and that this 'Book of the Twelve' contains two sections concerned with the destruction of Nineveh: Nahum and Jonah. In a sense they provide two sides of the same picture, Jonah asserts that forgiveness is possible even for those outside of Israel if only they repent. Nahum affirms that God will certainly punish even those outside of Israel if they do not repent. It may or may not be significant that Nahum and Jonah are the only two books in the whole of the Bible that end with a question.

A TASTER FROM NAHUM

Nahum 3:8–11

Are you better than Thebes, 8
  situated on the Nile, with water around her?
The river was her defence, the waters her wall.
Cush and Egypt were her boundless strength; 9
  Put and Libya were among her allies.
Yet she was taken captive and went into exile. 10
Her infants were dashed to pieces at the head of
  every street.
Lots were cast for her nobles, and all her great men
  were put in chains.
You too will become drunk; you will go into hiding 11
  and seek refuge from the enemy.

The destruction of Thebes, the ancient capital of Egypt situated on the Nile about 530 km south of Cairo, (where Luxor and Karnak stand today) would have been fresh in the minds of the Judeans as well as the Assyrians. If such a great city with such a great heritage could be conquered and destroyed, then there was no reason at all why the same thing could not happen even to Nineveh. Here was a warning for the Assyrians and an encouragement for the Judeans. It was sixty or seventy years since an earlier Assyrian commander had himself challenged the Judeans not to be over-confident: the gods of other nations had been powerless to deliver them from the Assyrian war-machine — why did they think that Yahweh could do any more (2 Kings 18:33–35)? In Nahum it is the Assyrians who are on the receiving end of such a challenge. The emphasis of the section is on the believability of Nineveh's fall: it really could happen. But here, as in the rest of the book the message goes further: Nineveh not only *could* be destroyed, she *will* be.

NAHUM FOR TODAY

It may at first sight seem that Nahum's blatant rejoicing at the thought of Assyria getting a taste of her own medicine is unacceptable or at least irrelevant for Christians today, in view of the New Testament teaching on forgiveness and the need to do good to our enemies. But although personal vengeance is never the right way forward, It may not necessarily be wrong to have a sense of vindication when cruelty and injustice are punished. Nahum at least raises that question for us. In point of fact, the New Testament in no way contradicts what Nahum has to say either about the sovereignty of God or about the fact that evil must and will be dealt with. Nahum certainly stands as a reminder that no regime, however powerful, is indestructible. It may even be felt as an encouragement to pray that the inevitable end of any such evil and oppressive regimes will come sooner rather than later. Nahum leaves no room for self-righteousness, but it does offer reassurance for those living under the shadow of present day 'Ninevehs'.

CHAPTER 15

Zephaniah

OUTLINE

ZEPHANIAH: THE MAN AND HIS TIME

According to 1:1 Zephaniah was prophesying during the reign of Josiah. Somewhat unusually, it also gives a

genealogy including four generations. This is probably
included to show that he was descended from king
Hezekiah, and thus a distant cousin of Josiah. However,
we cannot be certain that the Hezekiah mentioned is the
king, and it may be that the extra names are mentioned to
show Zephaniah's Judean roots because his father's name,
Cushi, could mean 'the Ethiopian'.

It seems likely that Zephaniah was the first writing
prophet after the long gap during the reign of Manasseh.
The dating of the prophecies depends on whether or not
the condemnation of Judah is seen as relating to the time
before Josiah's reforms have taken effect. On the one
hand, the star worship and other pagan practices mentioned
in chapter 1 were outlawed by Josiah. These references
would indicate a date prior to the reforms. On the other
hand, 1:4 mentions the 'remnant of Baal', which might
mean that action had already been taken against the Baal
cult. Similarly there is debate as to whether or not 2:13–15
implies that Nineveh has already fallen. If Zephaniah is to
be dated after the reforms then we have a further indication
that they were not very effective. However, his book does
not seem to reflect much hope for *national* repentance and
salvation as opposed to that of a small remnant. If he
wrote before the reforms and was himself one of the
influences encouraging Josiah to bring about the reforms,
his attitude seems rather defeatist. Overall, we cannot be
certain, but the balance of probability lies with the earlier
date, i.e. before 621 BC.

It has been suggested that the prophecy was prompted
by an invasion of Judah by the Scythians around 632 BC.
But although this invasion is mentioned by Herodotus,
there is a great deal of doubt about its timing and extent,
and its influence on Zephaniah is now largely discounted.
It has also been argued that the prophecy would have been
appropriate at the turn of the century during Jehoiakim's
reign, but there is no valid reason to reject the earlier
dating.

The text of Zephaniah presents a number of problems.

Several rare words and a number of unclear grammatical structures are used. The main sense of the book is plain but these difficulties are reflected in certain differences between the various translations.

THE PROPHECY

Zephaniah has many links with his contemporary, Jeremiah, and his writing clearly reflects a knowledge of earlier prophets like Micah and Isaiah. His work can be described as a summary of the teaching of the prophets on judgment and salvation. The book fits clearly into three sections. First comes a statement of warning and condemnation against the people of Judah, followed by a call to repentance. Second, there is an extension of this condemnation showing that while God's judgment certainly includes Judah it also extends over the whole world. The third section is a message of hope for those Judeans, 'the meek and humble, who trust in the name of the LORD', who will remain after the destruction of the rest and for whom the future will be a time of splendour bringing great joy to themselves and to God.

The message centres on the idea of the 'Day of Yahweh', a day when God's judgment will fall not only on the enemies of the covenant people but on Judah herself. Zephaniah picks up and develops the concept found in Amos 5 of the 'Day of the LORD' as a time to be feared rather than longed for. However, his message is not one of unadulterated gloom. He expresses no hope that the nation may avoid judgment, but he predicts that a small number of faithful people will be rescued and will live in a way that will be appropriate for the people of the covenant. It is very clear that as far as Zephaniah is concerned, both judgment and salvation are the work of Yahweh alone, whoever he may choose as instruments to effect his purposes.

A TASTER IN ZEPHANIAH

Zephaniah 2:1–3

Gather together, gather together,
   O shameful nation,
before the appointed time arrives   2
   and that day sweeps on like chaff,
   before the fierce anger of the LORD comes upon you,
   before the day of the LORD's wrath comes upon you.
Seek the LORD, all you humble of the land,   3
   you who do what he commands.
Seek righteousness, seek humility;
   perhaps you will be sheltered
   on the day of the LORD's anger.

The 'shameful nation' in verse 1 is not named. The initial
reference was almost certainly to the people of Jerusalem,
but the phrase has a universal application. There is a call
to take action before the day of judgment actually arrives.
The summons to 'gather together' is perhaps intended to
show that such action is more likely to be effective if it is
corporate. Zephaniah encourages them to meet together
and consider what is going on and what action they ought
to take, while there is still time. There is no suggestion,
however, that any action they take can prevent the judgment from happening. It is apparently too late for that.

It is significant that verse 3 does not call on the whole
nation to 'seek the LORD'. There may still be time for all
those who hear, to join 'the humble of the land', but
Zephaniah is apparently not optimistic that this will actually
happen. His message is chiefly for those who are already
seeking God's will. If they continue to do this, then
although the judgment is inevitable, they may be sheltered
from its worst effects. God's freedom is safeguarded here.
Even those who seek righteousness have no absolute
guarantee of personal safety. This verse has strong reminiscences of Micah 6:8 and God's requirement for the

people to 'act justly and to love mercy and to walk humbly with your God'.

ZEPHANIAH FOR TODAY

There may not be a great deal of original teaching in Zephaniah, but the reminders that he brought to the people of his time have a continuing relevance. For example, we note his conviction that God will not allow evil to continue unchecked and unpunished. There is a strong warning against complacency and the assumption of religious people that they have a special claim on God and will automatically avoid the effects of divine judgment. Zephaniah challenges all who leave God out of account and who think that whatever they do will have no effect on God's action or God's attitudes (1:12). God and his judgment must be taken seriously.

But taking God seriously also means recognizing him as the one who can bring restoration and cleansing. Chapter 3 contains a lovely picture of people from all nations being purified from their sins and serving Yahweh 'shoulder to shoulder' (v 9). The God whose power is shown in salvation and who can bring them safely through the day of judgment will then 'take great delight' in their company (v 17). Zephaniah thus portrays the two-way relationship with God that has been made impossible for the nation of Judah, as much as for the other nations, because of their idolatry and complacency but which will for a remnant one day be made possible by God himself. The New Testament offers a rationale of how, in Christ, this can happen.

CHAPTER 16

Habakkuk

OUTLINE

THE STRUCTURE OF HABAKKUK

It is difficult to analyse the book of Habakkuk in terms of
the literary forms of prophetic proclamation. The first two
chapters consist of a debate in which the prophet brings
before God his moral and spiritual problems about what

he can see happening in the world. This kind of direct questioning of God is not common in the prophetic books but it is often used in the Psalms (Pss 3, 10, 13, 22 etc.). Chapter 3 is a prayer or a psalm which has a separate heading and may have been written on a different occasion from the rest of the book. However, whether this is so or not, the whole book has a unified theme and the author or editor certainly intended the chapters to be treated together.

Habakkuk is in effect a theodicy, an attempted solution to the problem of how a God who is both just and sovereign can allow evil and suffering to continue apparently unabated in his world. The main literary problem in the book is deciding whether or not it is autobiographical, reflecting the prophet's personal struggles. The other suggestion is that it was composed as a cultic poem for use in the religious gatherings of the community. Chapter 3 includes musical directions at both beginning and end and, if not composed for public worship, must have been used in that context. The earlier chapters are clearly of pastoral value: they would be very helpful in encouraging and strengthening a community struggling with the problem of evil. But perhaps it is so helpful precisely because it expresses the conviction of the prophet who has wrestled with these matters personally, and has himself managed to find a way of coping with a life where such problems exist.

THE BACKGROUND TO HABAKKUK

The major clue to the dating of Habakkuk is found in 1:6. This mentions the Babylonians (literally 'Chaldeans', but they were the rulers in Babylon for quite a long period) as the tool God is going to use to punish the wicked in Judah. We are told that this was going to happen in the lifetime of the prophet but that it will be unexpected.

Politically, the major powers in the area over the last century had been Assyria and Egypt. Judah had for many years paid tribute to Assyria. The religious reforms of Josiah had entailed throwing off much of the Assyrian influence, but following his death in battle against the Egyptians (609 BC), Egypt then book overall control of Judah. Meanwhile, the power of Babylon had been growing remarkably quickly. First, the Babylonians destroyed Nineveh, the Assyrian capital (612 BC). Then they beat the Egyptians at the decisive battle of Carchemish (605 BC) and thus absorbed Judah in their sphere of influence. Judah's resistance to this take-over led Babylon to take action against Judah which eventually resulted in the exile and the destruction of Jerusalem in 587 BC.

In spite of the reforms of Josiah, little seems to have changed in Judah, morally, religiously and economically since the time of Micah. Habakkuk 1:3–5 tells us that the wicked were having things their own way and the authorities seemed powerless or unwilling to resist them.

It seems likely that Habakkuk was written during the latter part of Josiah's reign, or possibly shortly afterwards. Most scholars agree that it should be dated some time after the fall of Nineveh in 612 BC and before 597 BC, although it is possible that Habakkuk's surprise at the Babylonians being God's tool may indicate a date just before 612 BC.

THE AUTHOR

The prophet Habakkuk is not mentioned elsewhere in the Old Testament and the book says nothing about his background except that he was a prophet (*nabi*, 1:1; 3:19). This fairly common term only occurs as part of the heading of a prophetic book here, and in the post-exilic Haggai and Zechariah. Its use in this context may indicate that Habakkuk was a cultic prophet attached to the temple. The apocryphal 'Bel and the Dragon' (second century BC) contains a remarkable account of how Habakkuk was carried to Babylon by his hair so that he could deliver a meal to Daniel in the lion's den. Habakkuk is there described as 'the son of Joshua of the tribe of Levi', which, if it represents an accurate tradition, would support the view that Habakkuk was a prophetic teacher in the temple. The musical element in the book (3:1, 19) would reinforce this possible link with the temple.

From his book we see Habakkuk as a thoughtful person who takes seriously his responsibility to provide answers to the questions people bring (2:1b). He views life realistically and will neither accept nor supply easy answers to difficult questions about what he can see happening. He believes implicitly that God is both sovereign over the world and also just, but he struggles to reconcile this belief with his experience. His initial problem is the violence and injustice in the community. Why is God apparently doing nothing about it? The answer that God is going to use the Babylonians to punish the guilty is no help at all because the Babylonians are themselves guilty. To this further question God replies that the Babylonians too will eventually be dealt with, betrayed by their own pride. This does not really provide a logical answer to the moral problem of why a righteous God should use such wicked people in the first place, but it helps Habakkuk to stand firm in his own faith. The taunt song of 2:6–20 may be part of God's reply but it may be an emotional outlet for Habakkuk, enabling him to relieve his own feelings about Babylon before he makes his final prayer and statement of confident faith.

THE MESSAGE OF HABAKKUK

The teaching of Habakkuk can be summarized fairly easily. God is sovereign. God is just. Wickedness and sin may be tolerated for a while but they will be dealt with. Evil is in the end self-destructive; the unjust oppressor and his victims may think he has got away with his wrong-doing, but if they wait long enough he will perish. The faithful will be rewarded. God's presence can be known even when the circumstances of life are difficult.

However, the heart of the message of Habakkuk lies not

in its doctrine but in the pastoral help, the assurance and encouragement, it gives to those who are wrestling with the problems of life and faith. There are times when there seems to be no light at all, no evidence that God actually is at work in the world or even that he exists. In such circumstances there are only two paths a believer can take. One is to throw in his hand and deny his faith; the other is to keep on believing without proof. Habakkuk decides very positively to take the second route and writes his book in order to encourage his fellow Judeans to do the same. The key is perseverance. A long time may elapse before God shows his hand but in the meantime what is required is faithfulness: faith to believe that God will eventually intervene and also patient perseverance in continuing to live in God's way until he fully vindicates himself.

A TASTER IN HABAKKUK

Habakkuk 2:1–5

I will stand at my watch   1
    and station myself on the ramparts;
I will look to see what he will say to me,
    and what answer I am to give to this complaint.

The LORD's Answer
Then the LORD replied: 2
    'Write down the revelation
    and make it plain on tablets
    so that a herald may run with it.
For the revelation awaits an appointed time;   3
    it speaks of the end
    and will not prove false.
Though it linger, wait for it;
    it will certainly come and will not delay.
'See, he is puffed up;   4

his desires are not upright—
but his righteous will live by his faith—
indeed, wine betrays him;   5
he is arrogant and never at rest.
Because he is as greedy as the grave
and like death is never satisfied,
he gathers to himself all the nations
and takes captive all the peoples.

In chapter 1 Habakkuk has made his problems clear and
has questioned God in detail. God is too pure to even look
on evil; how does he tolerate and even make use of men
who are treacherous (1:13)?

In 2:1 we see Habakkuk waiting for God's answer. The
idea of the prophet as a watchman occurs also in Isaiah
21:8, Ezekiel 3:16–21; 33:1–9. Here the emphasis is twofold.
Firstly on the waiting until the answer is made clear; there
is an implicit assumption that an answer can be found and
will at some stage be revealed. (The situation is a familiar
one. The small child, when faced with the older versions
of the 23rd Psalm, may not understand why, if 'the Lord
is my shepherd', 'I shall not want' him, and yet accepts
that there must be an explanation of this puzzle!) Secondly
the emphasis is on standing firm, keeping on watch
during the time of waiting. If the prophet is going to help
in solving the problems of his people he must first be sure
of his own ground. At present he is not, so he waits for
God's vision to be given to him.

Verse 2 introduces God's reply. The last line of the verse
may mean '. . . so that whoever reads it may run with it'
leading to the NIV translation, 'that a herald may run with
it'. An alternative translation would be: 'that whoever
runs may read it' that is, it must be plain even to those
who can only spare a quick glance as they run by. In either
case the point is the same. The answer is to be written
down in such a way that everybody will be able to hear it
and understand it.

Verse 3 contains a warning that the 'revelation', the time
when the problem will be solved, the whole picture will

become clear and God's perspective revealed, may be a long time coming. But when the time is right there will be no more delay. However long God waits before acting, the believer need have no doubt that he will do so. Possibly, this verse actually forms the central part of the message and the following verses are added simply to indicate the possible course of events. On the other hand, verse 3 may still belong to the introduction and the key to the whole be found in vv 4–5.

The subject is omitted in the first line of verse 4, so we cannot be absolutely certain whether it is the wicked in Judah or the Babylonians who are being described as 'puffed up'. It is probably best to assume that the Babylonians are meant, though of course the ambiguity may be deliberate. The fate of the wicked is not explicitly spelt out until vv 6–20. But the implication is here, that although the unrighteous may seem to devour everything that comes in their way, their pride, and their greed for wine and for power will eventually betray them.

'The righteous will live by his faith'. Paul in Galatians 3:11 makes use of this verse to introduce a much fuller understanding of faith. The message here is that faithfulness, i.e. patient adherence to God's covenant, is what will enable them to keep going in these difficult circumstances.

HABAKKUK FOR TODAY

At first sight, Habakkuk may seem a book full of discouragement. It demands a realistic attitude about the world and its suffering. It speaks of times when those who believe in God do not understand what is happening and when he even appears to be going against his own nature. It raises all sorts of problems and provides no logical answers to them. But Habakkuk's experience is by no means unique and the purpose of his book is to provide encouragement to others who share his problems. It affirms that to seek understanding is not a crime and that it is right and proper to bring doubts and questions to God. There may be no easy answer to our difficulties but Habakkuk shows that waiting in God's presence for an answer is in itself worthwhile.

The Dead Sea Scrolls include a commentary on Habakkuk 1–2 which interprets Habakkuk solely in terms of the oppression suffered by the writer's own community sometime in the first or second century BC. This commentary does not shed much light on the original meaning and purpose of the text but it does help to show how relevant the book can be in different circumstances. At the end of his prayer in chapter 3 Habakkuk himself shows that the same principles apply whether the problem is injustice in society or the failure of the harvest. Patient and faithful perseverance is necessary in all circumstances. Hopeless situations need not lead to hopelessness. Even if the fig harvest, the grape harvest, the olive harvest and the wheat harvest all fail and the animals all die (or whatever is the industrial equivalent of this) it *is* still possible to trust and even to rejoice in the God who saves (3:17).

CHAPTER 17

Jeremiah

THE TIMES

We have already seen the general background to Jeremiah's ministry (pages 137–39) but if we are to understand the man and the book that bears his name we do need to know a little more about what was going on in and around the Judah of Jeremiah's day. It was a time of great political crisis in the Near East, and life and ideas in Judah were strongly affected by current developments.

Jeremiah was born at the end of Manasseh's reign, at a time when Assyria still had control of large sections of the Near East. Judah had become a vassal state of Assyria, and Manasseh had wholeheartedly embraced the debased Assyrian religion. It is important not to underestimate the extent of the apostasy, idolatry and moral corruption of this time (2 Kings 21). When Josiah came to the throne of Judah in 640 BC Assyria was beginning to have major problems nearer home and her hold over Judah was gradually last. Josiah instituted a series of reforms which were primarily religious, aiming to restore the nation to a life of obedience to Yahweh in accordance with the covenant made at Sinai. However, these reforms were also inevitably an expression of nationalism, one way of asserting independence of Assyria. In fact, although the long-term effect in terms of covenant obedience was negligible they did refocus national identity and pride.

In 612 BC the Assyrian capital fell to Babylon. In 609 BC the Egyptian armies moved north, apparently to support Assyria against her Babylonian enemies. Josiah, perhaps afraid that Assyrian control would be reasserted, attacked the Egyptian forces. He was killed in battle and Judah came under Egyptian control. Egypt herself was crushed by Babylon in 605 BC, and Judah then remained under Babylonian control; her various attempts at rebellion resulting only in first a partial and then a mass exile, and the destruction of Jerusalem in 587 BC.

The effect of Josiah's reforms did not long outlive him. After only three months on the throne, Josiah's son Jehoahaz was deposed by Egypt and replaced by his brother Jehoiakim. Jehoiakim made no attempt to continue Josiah's policies and was completely unmoved by Jeremiah's warnings (36:24) about the corrupt state of the nation. He died in 597 BC and his son Jehoiachin reigned for only three months before he became one of the early exiles to Babylon. Judah's last king, Zedekiah, had a number of problems in leadership, not least because many still saw Jehoiachin as the true king, and were expecting his speedy return from exile. Zedekiah refused to accept Jeremiah's advice that full submission to Babylon was the only viable policy; his refusal cost him dear (2 Kings 25:7). The accounts, found in Jeremiah and 2 Kings, of the fall of Jerusalem and the events leading up to it, are backed up by Babylonian Chronicles relating to the same times, and by a series of letters written on pieces of broken pottery which were discovered in the Israelite city of Lachish which also relate to the Babylonian invasion.

JEREMIAH THE MAN

His Background

Jeremiah came from the town of Anathoth, about 5 km NE of Jerusalem. His father's name was Hilkiah, and he belonged to a priestly family but we have no evidence that he himself ever practised as a priest. It is likely that he was descended from Abiathar the priest who had helped David at Nob and was himself descended from Eli. (See 1 Kings 2:26–27; Anathoth was a small town and it is unlikely that there were two priestly families living there.) If so, this would explain Jeremiah's interest in the fate of the sanctuary at Shiloh (7:12; 26:6).

We are not told anything of his upbringing, but it appears that he grew up in a family who resisted the excesses of Manasseh's reign. He was certainly given a good grounding in the Hebrew Scriptures, the Torah (the Pentateuch), the traditions and the prophets. He shows detailed knowledge of requirements which were laid upon Israel in the covenant agreement and his vocabulary and some illustrations he uses reflect a close awareness of the book of Hosea. It appears that Jeremiah's own family were later on not totally supportive of his work (12:6). This may have been, in part at least, because Jeremiah supported Josiah's reforms, which, with their stress on the centralization of worship in the temple and the removal of local shrines, could have threatened the livelihood of the priests of Anathoth.

He was called to be a prophet in 627 BC in the thirteenth year of Josiah's reign. It has been suggested that 1:5 implies that this was the year of Jeremiah's birth but it is generally accepted that he was around sixteen to eighteen years old at this time. This means that he must have known of the influences of Manasseh's reign although too young to experience them personally.

His Call

(cf. discussion of call narratives on p. 30)

Jeremiah's experience of God calling him to be a prophet had a very profound influence on his whole life. In some ways this calling constituted his own personal identity, and although at times he rebelled against it, it was something he could never escape. The written description of his call (1:4–19) appears to have been deliberately structured to reflect the account of the call of Moses in Exodus 3. It seems likely that Jeremiah, particularly as he encouraged the people to live in covenant relationship with God and condemned covenant breakers, saw himself as standing firmly in the tradition of Moses.

From the very beginning of his ministry Jeremiah was sure that he had been chosen to serve God in a special way even from before his birth. This conviction emphasized on the one hand the inevitability of his task and on the other, the way in which God planned and worked over a long period of time. Jeremiah was very conscious of his own inadequacy but, as Moses had been in the past, was reassured by God's promise to be with him. The sense of reluctance Jeremiah felt at his call apparently remained with him throughout his ministry, but so too did his consciousness that God's hand was on him and that God had a purpose for him and through him.

An important aspect of Jeremiah's call is the assurance that his message would be relevant not only for Judah but also for the nations (1:5). It would include a proclamation of judgment on Judah, involving great disaster brought about by the invasion of armed forces from the north (1:12–16). It would not be well received by his hearers and Jeremiah must therefore expect opposition (1:17–19). Yet it was not simply a message about uprooting and destruction, but also about planting and rebuilding (1:10).

His Life and Work

The book of Jeremiah gives such a strong impression of the character of the prophet that it is easy to forget how little we really know about his life. His call was in 627 BC and the accounts of his early preaching show it basically consisted of the call to repent in order to escape impending disaster. He appears to say nothing about Josiah's reforms, which were beginning to take place at this time, but it is likely that Jeremiah was both influenced by, and an influence on the reformation process. In 622 BC the book of the law was discovered in the temple (2 Kings 22). From then until Jehoiakim's reign began in 609 BC we have no record of any oracles from Jeremiah. One reason for this could be that Jeremiah stopped preaching while he waited to see what would result from Josiah's reforms. If the nation repented there would be no more need for his message of judgment. However, 25:3 does indicate that he continued preaching throughout this period; the reason why the oracles were not recorded may simply be that their content did not change.

From 609–587 BC we have plenty of information, although even the biographical material appears as fragments, in the recording of occasional events rather than a structured story. The 'temple sermon' mentioned in 26:1–6 and probably recorded in 7:2–15 appears to have marked a crisis in Jeremiah's ministry. Certainly from this point on, opposition appears to have intensified. The prophet was put in the stocks (20:2), banned from the temple (36:5), mocked and ostracized in various ways (17:15; 20:7) and eventually imprisoned (37:1 – 38:28).

The main reason for this was that his preaching was seen as both treasonable and blasphemous. Having realized that Josiah's reforms had done no more than scratch the surface, and national repentance was not going to be forthcoming, Jeremiah insisted that the only thing to do was to accept God's judgment and limit the damage by surrendering to the Babylonians. Inevitably this was seen as treason by the strongly nationalist government. Isaiah had said that Yahweh would not allow Jerusalem to fall (Isaiah 37:33–35). When Jeremiah warned that not only the city but even the great temple would be destroyed, the king's officers, in spite of the hypocrisy and disobedience in their own religious lives, denounced his message as blasphemy because it questioned the power of God and contradicted an oracle from Yahweh given through a recognized prophet from the past.

But Jeremiah was proved to be right. Jerusalem did fall,

the temple was looted, and large numbers of people were exiled. The Babylonians freed Jeremiah from prison and offered him the chance of accompanying the exiles to Babylon. He was convinced that God's purposes for Judah were going to be worked out through the exiles, but Jeremiah chose to remain behind in Jerusalem encouraging those who were left. Gedaliah, the governor appointed by Babylon and supported by Jeremiah, was murdered, and many of his troops were killed in an attempted coup. The coup failed, but the remaining soldiers lost their nerve and fled to Egypt for safety, forcing Jeremiah to go with them even though he insisted that this was futile. It is assumed that Jeremiah died in Egypt soon after this.

His Character

The book contains a number of intensely personal passages, rare in the prophetic writings, which read like sections from a private diary. In them, Jeremiah frankly displays his feelings and the way he himself struggled with his prophetic calling and in his own relationship with God. These passages, which include 11:18–23; 12:1–6; 15:10–12, 15–21; 17:14–18; 18:18–23; 20:7–13, 14–18, are often known as the 'confessions of Jeremiah'. It has been suggested that they were liturgical, written to be used as part of the temple worship services, but this seems highly unlikely. These 'confessions' mean that we know more of the character of Jeremiah than of any other prophet.

The picture that emerges is of a very complex man. There appears to have been a deep and continuing tension between Jeremiah's human desires and the situations his prophetic calling led him into. He longed for support and companionship, but the message he proclaimed brought him loneliness and rejection. He was even forbidden to marry (16:2). He was a great patriot, but was forced to proclaim that his country would be destroyed and to recommend immediate total surrender. He was deeply sensitive and very unsure of himself yet because his message was uncompromising, he seems to have come across to his compatriots as inflexible and hard-hearted.

He had a fierce hatred for Judah's sinful behaviour and a deep conviction that this would inevitably lead to disaster and destruction. He denounced his opponents in scathing terms, and yet, in spite of the suggestion that they were beyond prayer (7:16; 11:14), he continued to pray for them (18:20). At times he was driven to despair. He longed to escape from the consequences of his calling but could not. He felt deserted and deceived by God almost to the point of breakdown (15:15–18; 20:7, 14–18).

Although Jeremiah suffered so much personal anguish, it would be quite wrong to see his sense of depression and failure as the whole story. He believed in what he was doing, and was convinced that there was hope. The exile, although prolonged, would eventually come to an end and afterwards there would be a continuing future for Judah in her own land. He also found great consolation in his own personal relationship with God (15:16; 20:11).

JEREMIAH, THE BOOK

Its Structure and Composition

The book of Jeremiah can be described as a collection of writings by, about and related to, the work of the prophet Jeremiah. But it is very difficult to find any organizing principle by which the collection might have been arranged. It includes references to Jeremiah's work in four different reigns, but these are not arranged in chronological order. It includes three distinct types of material, poetic discourses, biographical details and prose sermons but they are not recorded in separate watertight sections. It is possible to trace a number of themes throughout the book but it does not seem to be arranged in thematic order. In short, it appears to be something of a hotch potch, an anthology of loosely connected writings.

Any investigation into how or why the collection might

have been brought together in this order is hampered by the fact that the book is available in two versions. In the Septuagint, (the Greek translation of the Old Testament), although in the rest of the text of Jeremiah the translation closely adheres to the Hebrew version, about twelve per cent is missing. Also the foreign nations oracles, found in the Hebrew from chapters 46–51, are in the Septuagint placed immediately after chapter 25 and their order is changed. Copies found at Qumran are somewhat closer to the Septuagint than to the Hebrew (Masoretic Text), and it does appear that the two versions were circulating separately at quite an early stage.

Nobody knows how these different versions arose. We do know that a number of documents were written by Jeremiah himself. A scroll giving an analysis of the first twenty three years of his ministry was produced in 605 BC (25:1ff; 36:1–32). This was written by Baruch, Jeremiah's secretary and friend, at Jeremiah's dictation. After Baruch had read it aloud in the temple, it was confiscated by the king's officers, read out to the king and then systematically cut up and destroyed by him. Jeremiah then dictated a revised and extended version of the same scroll. We cannot be certain about the contents of either of these scrolls, but it is likely that the material that they contained is embedded in chapters 1–25 of the book as we have it.

It is widely accepted that the poetic oracles come from Jeremiah himself. The biographical material must have been produced by a contemporary and is often assigned to Baruch. Some would see Baruch as responsible for collecting and preserving Jeremiah's own material and perhaps producing a first edition of the book. The prose sermons present more of a problem. They are closely tied in to the ideas and the language used in Deuteronomy and in the Deuteronomic history (Samuel and Kings). It has been suggested that these sermons were produced by an editor or a series of editors associated with the Deuteronomic school of thought responsible for Josiah's reforms. However, there are some differences from the Deuteronomic writings, and there is no conflict with Jeremiah's views as portrayed in the rest of the book. Perhaps these sections should be seen as edited versions of oral reports of Jeremiah's sermons.

Certainly Jeremiah is a complex book brought together over a period of time by a complex process, its final form being fixed some time during the period of exile. Because Jeremiah is at the heart of the whole book, it is a unity, but because it is an anthology it would be wrong to assume a logical development of thought. It is hard to define the purpose of the book as a whole and maybe it is a book for 'feeling' rather than for 'analysing'. However, the individual sermons, oracles and accounts do present very clear messages, all consistent with one another and together making a very powerful impact.

OUTLINE

1:1–3	Introductory statement
1:4–19	Jeremiah's call
2:1 – 3:5	Israel's behaviour and God's charges against them
3:6 – 4:4	Israel's unfaithfulness and a call to repentance
4:5 – 6:30	The coming disaster — proclamations and laments
7:1 – 9:26	God rejects Judah's hypocritical, idolatrous religion
10:1–16	Judah knows God's greatness, yet looks to idols!
10:17–25	Judgment is coming — prepare for exile
11:1–17	The covenant is shattered
11:18 – 12:17	A plot against Jeremiah, and his complaints to God
13:1–14	Illustrations for Jeremiah to use
13:15 – 17:27	The coming disasters: their certainty, their effect and their justification
18:1 – 19:15	Some lessons from spoiled and broken pottery
20:1–18	Jeremiah is persecuted and prays about it

THE TEACHING OF JEREMIAH

Jeremiah is firstly a preacher, only secondarily a writer, and in no sense a systematic theologian. Like all the prophets, his teaching comes in the context of messages given to particular people at particular times to meet particular situations. Although we shall be able to trace some major themes that recur consistently in the prophecy, it must be realized that such systematization in some ways does despite to the structure of the book as we have it.

Before attempting to analyse the teaching as a whole, it is helpful to read very carefully right through one or two of Jeremiah's sermons in order to get an impression of the way he preached. In particular the 'temple sermon' of 7:1–29 serves as a good summary of the key aspects of his prophecy. Here Jeremiah castigates the people of Judah for committing major violations of the covenant law while at the same time assuming that their national identity was safeguarded by the trappings of their formal religion. He makes it clear that obedience not traditions and ritual is the essence of faith, and he proclaims God's judgment on Judah.

God's Character

His understanding of the character and nature of God is basic to all of Jeremiah's preaching but in most instances it is assumed rather than explicitly proclaimed. Monotheism, for example, is pre-supposed and the question of the possible existence of other gods is nowhere at issue. His understanding is grounded both in his training in the law and covenant traditions and in his own personal experience. Jeremiah knows Yahweh as the sovereign God, who created the universe and is in control of all that is (5:22; 8:7; 27:5–6; 32:17). Because God is sovereign he is also free, free even to change his mind (18:7–12). God is portrayed as full of compassion and loyal love, always willing to respond to repentance with deep forgiveness (3:12; 9:24; 31:3, 20; 33:11). But he is also just and righteous and will be uncompromising in his judgment on the evil and unrepentant (9:25–26; 44:2–6). God knows and understands human beings and he holds them fully accountable for their behaviour (11:20; 18:10; 20:12; 29:23). God's requirements are set out in 9:23–24 in a way that is reminiscent of Micah 6:8.

God is both transcendent, 'wholly other' than mankind, the one who fills heaven and earth, and also immanent, the God who is 'nearby' (23:23–24). His ways are not always easy to understand. The prophet himself talks of being deceived by God, and on many occasions appears to have been puzzled by the way things were going (20:7–8; 32:17–25). He knew by experience that God would not keep him from suffering. But his experience also taught him that God was totally approachable; Jeremiah never shows any hesitation in bringing his anguished complaints and questions to God, always expecting him to listen and respond.

The People of God

Jeremiah had a clear understanding of what Yahweh expected from Judah as his covenant people. They were to live in relationship to God and obey his commands (11:1–5). Although the ritual commands relating to sacrifice and the temple were important, they were meaningless without personal commitment. What God really wanted was a people who understood what he was like, who shared his interests and who reflected his kindness, justice and righteousness in their daily lives (9:23–24). If their daily lives and relationships were not grounded in the covenant then they might as well go ahead and break all the ritual laws as well, because God hated what they are doing: obedience rather than ritual was the bottom line (7:21–23).

Jeremiah gives an equally clear picture of what Judah actually was like and how far short the nation fell of God's requirements. It seems that Josiah's reforms had led to an increased level of cultic activity (6:20; 7:21) but Jeremiah also perceived an increase in the extent of their rebellion against God with no signs of genuine repentance (7:1–5; 8:4–9). They were deeply involved in idolatry and immorality (2:23–25; 7:30–33; 5:1–9) and their leadership was corrupt. Prophets and priests served their own interests, they were willing knowingly to deceive the people and appeared to encourage syncretism (7:3–11; 8:10–17; 14:11–16; 23:9–40). The monarchy too came under Jeremiah's con-

demnation because the kings rejected their responsibilities
(21:11 – 22:9). Throughout society he saw the same hypocrisy and rebellion against God (5:1–9).

One major problem Jeremiah faced was in Judah's
distorted view of herself and of God's requirements. The
negative response to his preaching was grounded in a
refusal to acknowledge the truth of the picture he drew of
the nation or of the way in which he presented God's
demands. People believed that because Yahweh had made
a covenant with Israel and had given them the temple in
Jerusalem, he was committed to them unconditionally: he
simply would not allow the nation to be destroyed. All
that was needed was to ensure that the Yahwistic rituals
were carried out; if these were performed then it really did
not matter what else was done. On this basis the prophets
and priests kept proclaiming God's peace to the people as
if the way they were living did not matter (6:13–15; 8:10–12).
But Jeremiah knew it was not possible for new life to be
given to Judah until these false hopes were destroyed and
they learned to trust in Yahweh himself rather than in
ritual and tradition and also to obey him.

The temple in which they had placed such faith was
already doomed. What mattered now was that the people
of Judah understood the significance of this in terms of
their own sin and God's judgment on it. In no way did it
mean that God was powerless to protect them.

The Future

There was no question in Jeremiah's mind, or at least not
in his preaching, about what kind of short and medium-
term future awaited Judah. Failing a major change of heart
(and Jeremiah soon realized that that was unlikely if not
impossible (6:27–30)), then disaster and destruction were
inevitable. At first this appears as a rather vague picture
of an enemy coming from the north (1:14–16). It is just
possible that there was a threat of a Scythian invasion
during Josiah's reign which prompted these prophecies,

but although the Scythians were undoubtedly causing problems for a weakening Assyria there is no evidence that they ever threatened Judah. In any case, this generalized depiction of a northern enemy gradually focused into a clear image of this enemy. It was the Babylonians who were God's chosen means of judgment.

As the Assyrian threat receded and Josiah was even able to regain some of the former Israelite territory the impression grew that Jeremiah's early warnings had been overstated. He was seen as a scaremongering irrelevance. But in spite of the temporary relief, Jeremiah was convinced that things would get much worse before there could be any possibility of a future for Judah in their own land. God had withdrawn his blessing (16:5). The monarchy, the city of Jerusalem and the temple would all be lost and the population exiled for a considerable time (25:1–38; 27:1–22; 29:10).

Jeremiah's call, however, had been not only to tear down, but also to build up. As Judah's situation grew worse, and Jeremiah's warnings began to appear very realistic, his own hope and vision for the future gained strength. He was convinced that God still had a long-term purpose for Judah which would be worked out through the exiled community. In his letter to the exiles (29:1–32), he explained that although they would definitely be in Babylon for many years, nevertheless God had great plans for a repentant and cleansed community, settled once more in their own land. On God's instructions, Jeremiah showed his own faith in the future by buying a piece of land (32:1–15). This was a sign to the people that the long exile would one day come to an end and normal business procedures of buying and selling land would be restored. In general Jeremiah's vision for the future included prosperity within the land. Basic to it was a restored relationship with God including wholehearted, righteous worship (chs 30–31, 33); twice we find a hint that there may even be a place for Gentiles (16:19; 30:8–9). Certainly it entailed the coming of a new Davidic king and the institution of a completely new covenant (30:9; 31:33–34; 33:15–18).

The New Covenant

Jeremiah's personal experience shaped one of his most far-reaching prophecies. He had been saddened by the hollowness of Josiah's official reformation of the cultus. He had become only too well aware of how deep-seated was the sin and rebellion against God which lay at the root of human nature. While he was convinced of God's deep love for the people he was also strongly aware of God's holiness. Above all, he knew from experience that it was possible to have a real and personal relationship with God. Perhaps it was because of these factors that Jeremiah began to speak particularly to individuals. People could not simply blame their leaders, nor society as a whole. Each person mattered and it was as individuals that they were responsible to God for what they did. Jeremiah could see that the most urgent need was the transformation of individual lives from within.

It was this awareness of the need for transformed lives, a sense that somehow the old covenant had not fulfilled that need and the conviction that God had not yet finished with or given up on his people that moulded Jeremiah's thinking and led to his teaching about the New Covenant (31:31–40). A time would come when God would relate to his people in a new way. Time and time again they had broken the old covenant with its laws written at Sinai on stone tablets. So this time God's law would be written on their hearts. People would serve and obey God by nature. They would know God's will not because a prophet or the sanctuary priest has explained it to them, but because they were themselves in touch with God. Thanks to this close personal relationship with Yahweh, even the Ark of the Covenant will be unnecessary (3:16). It has been suggested that these verses simply mean that in the future every Jew will know God's law by heart and understand its meaning. But it is difficult to believe that Jeremiah is referring to rote learning. Jeremiah makes it clear that religion is to be defined in terms of direct personal knowledge; knowing 'by heart' the LORD rather than the law (9:24; 24:7).

The 'Righteous Branch'

Closely connected with his teaching on the New Covenant is Jeremiah's messianic hope. He spoke of a coming descendant of David, a 'righteous branch, a King who will reign wisely and do what is just and right in the land' (23:5–6; 33:15–16). Thus Jeremiah's vision of individual salvation and a personal relationship with God is linked to traditional ideas of the Messiah and also involves the community (cf 31:35). To some extent these prophecies of hope do relate to the time of return after the exile, but they also look further into the future. It is noteworthy that these New Covenant ideas are never presented in the Old Testament as anything other than a prophecy of future events. Hebrews 10 sees this prophecy as being fulfilled by the events of the New Testament; indeed Jesus himself speaks of his own work in terms of the new covenant (Matthew 26:28; Luke 22:20).

Foreign Nations

Other than in the foreign nations oracles of chapters 46–51 Jeremiah says little about what will happen to the nations outside Israel. The universal extent of God's power over the nations is clearly affirmed, e.g. in 25:9 and 27:6, where Nebuchadnezzar is described as the servant of Yahweh. That the nations will come under God's judgment is equally clear; 46–51 are in effect statements about the extent of that judgment. Babylon in particular, in spite of being God's instrument to punish Israel, is in the final resort denounced as God's enemy and her eventual destruction is declared to be certain; she will 'sink to rise no more' (51:64). There is little evidence of a universal hope for the nations, although 16:19 and 30:8–9 could be interpreted as involving Gentiles in Judah's future new life. The most positive statements about the nations are in 12:15–17 and 16:19–21: if foreign nations

who have been exiled from their own lands because of
God's judgment will recognize Yahweh's hand in their
circumstances and learn from God's people, then they too
can be restored.

Illustrations and Symbolic Actions

Like Amos and Hosea, Jeremiah makes considerable use
of symbols and pictures to reinforce his teaching. His
remaining unmarried, for example had symbolic significance, just as had Hosea's marriage to an adulterous
woman. On one occasion Jeremiah took a waistcloth and
buried it by the river (13:1–11). When he returned some
time later the cloth was, not surprisingly, ruined. This
pictured the way in which Judah, although like a waistcloth
it should have been fastened tightly to God, had become
useless. Another time, Jeremiah went around wearing a
yoke (27:1–11) trying to explain how real would be the
control that Babylon was to have over Judah. We have
already seen how he bought a piece of land to show
confidence in the future (32:1–15).

Not all his illustrations were acted out. Among the best
known is the picture in 18:1–11 of God as the potter and
Judah as the clay. If the pot was flawed or misshapen then
the potter would reshape the clay into something different.
Thus Judah must be completely re-moulded before the
nation could again function as God's people (cf 19:10–11).
He also derives imagery from marriage (2:2; 3:1–13; 31:22),
almond blossom (1:11–12), pots boiling over (1:13–14) and
baskets of figs (24:1–10). In every case Jeremiah's illustrations and symbolic actions were accompanied by an
explanation of their meaning. Such actions were teaching
aids. They were not some kind of sympathetic magic, as
if by smashing a jar which represented Jerusalem, Jeremiah
himself brought about the destruction of the city (19:1–13);
but they got across the point in a very forceful way.

TASTERS IN JEREMIAH

Jeremiah 5:1–5

'Go up and down the streets of Jerusalem,
   look around and consider,
   search through her squares.
If you can find but one person
   who deals honestly and seeks the truth,
   I will forgive this city.
Although they say, "As surely as the LORD lives",   2
   still they are swearing falsely.'
O LORD, do not your eyes look for truth?   3
   You struck them, but they felt no pain;
   you crushed them but they refused correction.
They made their faces harder than stone
   and refused to repent.
I thought, "These are only the poor;   4
   they are foolish,
for they do not know the way of the LORD,
   the requirements of their God.
So I will go to the leaders and speak to them;   5
   surely they know the way of the LORD,
   the requirements of their God."
But with one accord they too had broken off the yoke
   and torn off the bonds.'

Here we have an example of Jeremiah's poetic ability. The form of the passage is a debate between Yahweh and the prophet. Even in the English translation the depth of personal feeling and involvement comes across as the sin of the nation is discussed. This section is an explanation of and justification for the judgment, described in the preceding and succeeding sections, which God is going to bring on Judah through the northern enemy.

Verses 1 and 2 are reminiscent of Abraham's discussion with God about possible forgiveness for Sodom (Genesis 18:16–33). Forgiveness would be possible for Judah and

Jerusalem even at this late stage but there is no possible basis on which it could be granted. There is plenty of official worship and acknowledgment of Yahweh, but all of it is hypocritical. Verse 3 is an indication that this passage was written late in Josiah's reign or early in Jehoiakim's. The reforms had already taken place but had been shown to have had no real effect in changing the hearts and lives of the people. They still believed that external forms of worship were enough. But God requires truth. It was inconceivable to Jeremiah that they had not grasped that fact, that their knowledge of God's nature was so limited.

They had been given many chances to repent but had deliberately refused to do so. It is clear that there can be no excuse for their behaviour, but Jeremiah tries to find one. Surely it could only be the uneducated, those who have had no opportunity to know anything of the law, who could possibly behave in this way? But no, 'with one accord' the leaders too had deliberately broken the covenant. There was no way, therefore in which the covenant curses could be prevented from coming into play.

Jeremiah 16:19–21

O LORD, my strength and my fortress,   19
   my refuge in time of distress,
to you the nations will come
   from the ends of the earth and say,
"Our fathers possessed nothing but false gods,
   worthless idols that did them no good.
Do men make their own gods?   20
   Yes, but they are not gods!"
"Therefore I will teach them—   21
   this time I will teach them
   my power and might.
Then they will know that my name is the LORD.

This brief oracle concerning foreign nations seems to be

separate from the surrounding context. It has been suggested that this is in fact an editorial insertion written
during the exile, but a number of the phrases are used
elsewhere by Jeremiah himself and there is no compelling
reason to believe that he would not have written about the
nations in this way. The section begins with a reference
to Jeremiah's own relationship to Yahweh: he knows
Yahweh as dependable and as providing security in difficult
times. This leads to an assertion that even pagan nations
will come to Yahweh, recognizing his uniqueness and the
worthlessness of their own so-called gods. If verse 21 also
refers to the nations then the implication is that in the end
they too will be taught by Yahweh and will know his
name, that is, will understand his character. However, it
is possible that verse 21 refers to Judah.

In this case, the meaning is that just as Jeremiah and
the nations acknowledge what God is like, so Judah also,
by the exercise of God's power in judgment, will be
brought to understand what the name of Yahweh signifies.

Jeremiah 38:7–13

But Ebed-Melech, a Cushite, an official in the royal   7
    palace, heard that they had put Jeremiah into the
    cistern. While the king was sitting in the Benjamin
    Gate,
Ebed-Melech went out of the palace and said   8
    to him,
'My lord the king, these men have acted wickedly   9
    in all they have done to Jeremiah the prophet.
They have thrown him into a cistern, where he will
    starve to death when there is no longer any bread
    in the city.'
Then the king commanded Ebed-Melech the   10
    Cushite, 'Take thirty men from here with you and
    lift Jeremiah the prophet out of the cistern before
    he dies.'
So Ebed-Melech took the men with him and went   11

to a room under the treasury in the palace. He took
some old rags and worn-out clothes from there and
let them down with ropes to Jeremiah in the cistern.
Ebed-Melech the Cushite said to Jeremiah, 'Put   12
these old rags and worn-out clothes under your
arms to pad the ropes.' Jeremiah did so,
and they pulled him up with the ropes and lifted   13
him out of the cistern. And Jeremiah remained
in the courtyard of the guard.

This straightforward account speaks for itself but no
account of the book of Jeremiah should overlook the
biographical 'snapshots'. This delightful account of how
Ebed-melech rescued Jeremiah from certain death after he
had been thrown into an empty water-storage pit, confirms
the picture of the king, Zedekiah, as indecisive and
responding to whoever spoke to him last. It also reminds
us that there were a few good-hearted people left in Judah
even if only, as in Ebed-melech's case, amongst the
immigrant population.

JEREMIAH FOR TODAY

The New Testament contains some forty direct quotations
from Jeremiah and although about half of these occur in
Revelation in connection with the fall of Babylon, the
overall number is an indication of how valuable the book
can be.

Before we examine the contemporary relevance of this
diverse collection, it is worth considering its significance
for the Babylonian exiles. They might have regarded its
message as depressing and discouraging; a kind of divinely
sanctioned 'I told you so' which rubbed salt in the wound.
However, though Jeremiah himself seems never to have
been really at peace with his own prophecies, he did help
the nation to understand and therefore to survive the
catastrophe which had befallen them. The official cult

personnel could supply no answer. They had simply taken it for granted that Yahweh would never allow such a thing to happen. But it had happened. Their only possible response could be either to assume that Yahweh was not in fact all-powerful, or else that he had cast them off for ever and then, in either case, to sink into despair. But precisely because Jeremiah had already demonstrated the weakness of their theology, his message of judgment became part of a message of hope and salvation for the future. As John Bright puts it: 'By ruthlessly demolishing false hope, by ceaselessly asserting that the tragedy was Yahweh's doing, his righteous judgment on the nation for its sin, Jeremiah as it were drew the national disaster within the framework of faith, and thus prevented it from destroying faith' (*Jeremiah* The Anchor Bible, Doubleday 1965).

Simply because Jeremiah is such a varied anthology it is not easy to speak of the relevance of the book as a whole, as opposed to the insights offered by individual passages. But there are a number of points which are brought out very clearly and deserve attention.

i. Jeremiah, particularly in his early preaching registers his own sense of shock at his nation's apostasy, ingratitude and sheer wickedness. It is vital that we retain the capacity to be shocked by evil. It is very easy to take sin and evil for granted and to become very blasé about what should fill us with horror. But to do this is to seriously under-estimate the meaning of God's holiness, and his purpose for humankind.

ii. Anyone who claims to speak for God must be willing to proclaim bad news as well as good. But Jeremiah shows that preaching bad news is a very painful procedure for the preacher. There is room for despair, but none for revelling in the proclamation of judgment on other people, however much we may detest what they stand for.

iii. God's sovereignty is as real today as it was in the time of Jeremiah. God is still involved in the lives of nations, and of individuals even from before their birth, and God's plans and purposes will be worked out. How-

ever, the fact that God is sovereign means that he is free
to act as he wills: Jeremiah provides a strong warning
against a short-sighted theology that would like to force
God to act in the 'correct' way and in consequence has no
answer when things work out differently. Both Jeremiah
and his opponents recognized that God was committed to
the Davidic covenant and Jeremiah was criticized for
suggesting that certain things which were seen as part and
parcel of that covenant could ever be destroyed. What his
short-sighted opponents did not see was that God's commitment to the Davidic covenant was being worked out in
quite a different way from what they had imagined, so
that their trust in the external forms was completely
misplaced.

iv. Jeremiah shows us that God can use all kinds of
different characters, sensitive depressives as well as confident extroverts. At the same time he provides us with an
example of the kind of close personal relationship that it
is possible to have with God. A relationship that demands
absolute obedience and yet allows questioning and debate.
A relationship that involves trust and brings security and
yet provides no guarantee at all of freedom from suffering.
In this respect, Jeremiah is a forerunner of the New
Testament teaching that the one who is closest to God,
who is most in accord with God's will is the one who is
likely to suffer the most. It is interesting to see how many
parallels there are between Jeremiah and Jesus. Jeremiah,
too, was like a lamb led to the slaughter and it is perhaps
not surprising that some people thought that Jesus was
Jeremiah returned (Matthew 16:14). Jeremiah shows us
that even in despair it is possible to serve God faithfully
and well and that when people do this God provides help
to endure (if not ways to escape from) situations in which
it would be easy to despair.

v. Jeremiah's teaching on the New Covenant, particularly
when taken in conjunction with the way it is developed
in the letter to the Hebrews offers a profound understanding of what was involved in the coming of Jesus and of a

distinctively Christian relationship with God. This entails the provision of a new dynamic, which guarantees the human side of the covenant as well as God's. Thus the New Covenant offers a confidence and a security that were not available to Jeremiah under the Old Covenant.

Obadiah

OUTLINE

BACKGROUND

Obadiah is the shortest of the books in the Old Testament; with its 21 verses it is not even considered long enough to divide into chapters. We know nothing of the prophet. It is possible that he had a much wider ministry and this was the only one of his oracles to be preserved; on the other hand his prophetic work may have been limited to this one message against Edom. It has been suggested that the book is in any case not a record of a single speech but a collection of short units. One reason for this suggestion is the apparent connection between Obadiah and passages in Jeremiah 49, Ezekiel 25, Psalm 137 and Joel 2. Jeremiah 49:9 and Joel 2:32 in particular seem to have direct links with Obadiah 5 and 17. However, while Obadiah may have used other sources referring to Edom there is no real reason to doubt that this prophecy forms a unity that was put together on one occasion.

Our ignorance about Obadiah himself is one reason why the prophecy is also difficult to date. According to Malachi 1:3, Edom was destroyed by the middle of the fifth century, so Obadiah cannot be dated later than that. It is possible that Jeremiah quotes from Obadiah rather than the other way round, so that the actions of Edom referred to here relate to some earlier attack such as the ones described in 2 Chronicles 21 or 2 Chronicles 28. However, the description of Jerusalem's fate does seem to tie in with the exile to Babylon in 587 BC, and since the strength of feeling displayed may well indicate that this is an eye-witness account, it may be best to date the prophecy soon after that time.

In spite of these uncertainties the general picture is clear. The people of Edom, who as descendants of Esau might be regarded as brothers of the Israelites, had behaved in a most unbrotherly fashion! In fact, although the brotherhood between these two nations is mentioned on a number of occasions, (Deuteronomy 23:7–8; Amos 1:11), for most of their history their relationship seems to have been hostile. In this particular instance it seems that Edom was not the primary enemy but when Judah was under attack from elsewhere and about to go under, Edom not only gloated over their fate but took every opportunity to hasten their demise, to leap in to occupy their territory and to plunder their goods. Both their attitude and their behaviour merited judgment.

THE MESSAGE OF OBADIAH

It is important to remember that Obadiah's prophecy was actually a message for Judah rather than for Edom. This pattern of presenting an oracle addressed to one nation but actually aimed at a different set of people is a common technique in prophetic writing. If the sixth century dating is correct the message is directed to a disheartened and

disillusioned group of exiles, only too aware that they
have wasted their opportunities and rightly received God's
judgment; although Obadiah does not actually raise the
question of Judah's guilt. A particular source of discouragement was the thought that not only were the sins of other
nations apparently remaining unpunished, but that these
nations were also rejoicing at Judah's downfall. Judah was
helpless to change her situation, but Obadiah's words will
have been a source of comfort and encouragement. In very
vivid terms he expressed the way they were feeling, and
made it clear that Edom too would be destroyed. He also
offered Judah a promise of eventual restoration. God had
not singled them out for punishment, and however black
the present might be, there was hope for the future.

The fate of Edom is described in graphic terms. The
destruction envisaged for them is complete. It will dwarf
the damage normally done by thieves and marauders. As
they had taken advantage of Judah's humiliation, so other
nations will exploit Edom's misfortune, so much so, that
she will be wiped out.

It has been suggested that Edom is here regarded as
'typical' of Judah's enemies; a specific instance reinforcing
the general prophetic teaching that God is active in the
world however much appearances might seem to contradict the fact, and that all who oppose God's will, will
eventually receive their due reward.

OBADIAH FOR TODAY

We may well wonder what possible relevance these few
verses can have for today. Behind Obadiah's words are
two important assumptions. One is that God's people are
not exempt from troubles. They must not assume, any
more than Judah could, that God will prevent 'Edomites'
from causing them harm. Secondly, there is the underlying
conviction that we are all, even if we make no claim to
follow God, answerable to him for the way we treat our
fellow men and women. Injustice and gloating over the

misfortunes of others are still common today; nations still take advantage of the misfortunes of their fellows. Obadiah affirms that it is equally true that God is still at work so that in the end the balance will be restored and justice will both be done and be seen to be done. The New Testament gives a different perspective on Obadiah's confident conclusion 'And the kingdom will be the LORD's', but its validity and the encouragement we can gain from it remain.

Jonah

OUTLINE

Even a quick glance makes it clear that the book of Jonah is unlike the other prophetic books. Several of these contain narrative sections describing certain events that have happened to the prophets, but in Jonah the whole book, with the possible exception of the psalm in chapter 2, is in narrative form. The only actual prophetic proclamation (3:4), consists of precisely eight words (translating only five words in Hebrew): 'Forty more days and Nineveh will be overturned'. Clearly the message of the book is contained not in the preaching of the prophet but in the story itself. It is important therefore, that before considering those lessons and even before looking at some of the problems raised by the book, we take a close look at the story in these four short chapters.

THE STORY OF JONAH

Jonah the son of Amittai is mentioned only once in the Old Testament outside of this book. 2 Kings 14:25 says that in the time of Jeroboam II of Israel, a successful campaign to win back territory was prophesied by Jonah who came from the town of Gath Hepher, near Nazareth. The book of Jonah itself, however, makes no reference at all to any activity by Jonah in Israel; it begins with God commanding Jonah to go and preach against the 'great city' of Nineveh. Nineveh was the capital of the Assyrian Empire and had a well-deserved reputation for terrible cruelty and oppression, so it would be easy to understand why God had come to the end of his patience and decided to exercise judgment on them. There are reminiscences here of the 'outcry' against Sodom and Gomorrah described in Genesis 18–19 (compare Genesis 18:20f with Jonah 1:2).

Jonah responds to this call to proclaim judgment on Nineveh by running in the opposite direction! It is difficult to understand at first why he should do this; surely an Israelite would be only too pleased that God was going to do something about Nineveh's wickedness. But we should note that although many prophetic books include judgment oracles against foreign nations, almost all of those are delivered to Israel or to Judah, encouraging them with a promise that their enemies will be defeated. Jonah, by contrast is asked to go to Nineveh and proclaim a message of judgment there. As a prophet he realized that the point of a proclamation of judgment was to give the hearers the opportunity of repenting and thus avoiding the judgment. Jonah just could not cope with the thought that Nineveh, after committing so many atrocities, might respond to his message and avoid the punishment which, he agreed, they deserved. 4:1–2 make it clear that this is why Jonah reacted as he did.

Jonah's flight is described in some detail. He boarded a ship heading for Tarshish (possibly located in Spain) which in the course of its voyage encountered a terrible storm. The author's literary skill can be seen in the way tension builds within the chapter, as the growing strength of this storm is paralleled by the growing terror of the sailors. These sailors, apparently from different places and worshipping different gods, began to plead desperately each with their own deity. Since every possible prayer was needed, Jonah could not be allowed to sleep on; his prayer might be the decisive factor. But all the prayers went unanswered and the storm continued. So further measures were taken in order to discover whether there might be somebody on board who was responsible for this disaster and 'the lot fell on Jonah' (1:7).

Jonah's statement of faith in this context is both clear and, in the circumstances, somewhat ironic. (The author's humour surfaces in the book on a number of occasions.) The God that Jonah worshipped, he told them, the one whom, (as they already knew) he had taken this voyage to avoid, was the LORD, Yahweh, the supreme God who made the land and the sea and who therefore cannot be avoided. No wonder the superstitious sailors were afraid. Jonah's request, at this point, to be thrown into the sea may reflect a genuine desire to save the sailors' lives, but understood in the context of the book as a whole it may represent a further stage in Jonah's ongoing battle with God. He could have asked to be returned to where he came from but he preferred to die rather than have anything to do with a mission that might end with the Ninevites being forgiven.

The portrayal of the sailors as good-hearted people in spite of being pagans is probably deliberate. They did their best to save Jonah, but in the end agreed to his request to throw him overboard. The storm stilled and the sailors acknowledged the power of Yahweh, the God whom Jonah worshipped. It may be inappropriate to interpret 1:16 as implying formal conversion, but nevertheless irony reappears at this point. Even in avoiding God's commission to preach to pagans Jonah was responsible for bringing other pagans to acknowledge God.

The irony is not over; Jonah had hoped to die but the sovereign God had other plans and through the intervention of a great fish, delivered him safely to dry land. Although it features prominently in retellings of the story of Jonah, the great fish (not a whale!) receives little attention in the book, being simply the means God used to return Jonah to his starting place. Once in the fish, Jonah realized that he was not quite so keen to die as he had thought, and turned to God, recognizing, in the final line of the psalm he used, that 'Salvation is of the LORD'. However, later chapters present a prophet who is was still a long way from realizing the intensity of God's desire to save and the breadth of God's concerns. The prayer in chapter 2 does not refer directly to Jonah's circumstances; it is a song of praise after deliverance rather than a prayer for deliverance. The terminology used quotes freely from other known psalms (eg Psalms 88:6; 42:7; 30:3; 11:4; 42:4), and it may be that Jonah recites a remembered song. On the other hand the language, with its increasing despair and its references to the deep waters, fits very easily into this context and could well have been composed by Jonah himself.

Recommissioned without argument, Jonah rather grudgingly accepts the task and delivers his very brief message. To his regret, though not really to his surprise, the people do respond and in an attempt to avoid the threatened judgment make an effort to change their ways. This is enough to arouse God's ready compassion and the threat of destruction is withdrawn. We note that the Ninevites seem to be accused of general crimes against humanity, which as Amos 1 and 2 make very clear, God will not tolerate. Their response involves recognizing their sin and discontinuing some of their violence in an attempt to appease God. There is not even a hint here of the recognition seen among the sailors that Jonah's God, the LORD, is sovereign, and certainly no indication of a whole-hearted turning to Yahweh.

One might have expected the story to end there. But although Jonah had carried out God's will, he was still a long way from understanding and accepting it. The central focus of the story is not so much the mercy God showed to Nineveh and his compassionate decision to spare the city

but rather the way in which Jonah understood and reacted
to events. It is often suggested that chapters 1–2 deal with
the salvation of Jonah and chapters 3–4 with the salvation
of Nineveh, but the truth is that even after being saved
from the great fish, Jonah still needed to be delivered from
his own selfishness and prejudice.

In chapter 4 the ongoing debate between God and Jonah
is brought out into the open. Jonah is really angry and
tells God so in no uncertain terms. His anger may result
in part from having been shown up as a fool or a false
prophet because the judgment he had predicted had not
happened. However the root of the problem seems to be
that God had showed compassion on a city like Nineveh.
If such a city could 'get away with it', what, Jonah
demanded, was the point in life? He may as well be dead.

Once more the irony in the book surfaces. Even while
he berates God, Jonah shows a clear intellectual knowledge
of what God was like. He recites the familiar credal
formula: 'You are a gracious and compassionate God, slow
to anger and abounding in love, a God who relents from
sending calamity' (4:2). Jonah's problem was that he had
no sympathy with God's purposes in the world and in no
sense shared God's compassion. In the rather strange
incident of the fast-growing vine and the destructive
worm Jonah was brought face to face with the selfishness
of his own concerns and with the justification of God's
concern for Nineveh. The book, like Nahum, ends with a
question, 'Should I not be concerned about that great
city?'. The reader is left in no doubt concerning the right
answer to that question. But the fact that Jonah's answer
goes unrecorded compels readers to formulate their own
response.

SOME LITERARY CONSIDERATIONS

Authorship and Dating

The book, written in the third person except where

Jonah's own words are being quoted, is anonymous, and we have no clues to indicate who the author might be. The Jonah of 2 Kings 14, lived in the eighth century so the book cannot have been produced before then, but it may have been written much later than that. Some scholars suggest that 3:3 indicates that Nineveh was no longer in existence at the time of writing and argue for a date after 612 BC when Nineveh was destroyed. Others think that the whole point of the book would have been lost if Nineveh had already been destroyed and that therefore it must have been written before 612 BC. The use of certain Hebrew terms could indicate a later date but we cannot be absolutely sure.

Historical Accuracy

What sort of a book is Jonah? Earlier suggestions that Jonah may be mythological or allegorical are now largely discounted but we need to consider whether Jonah should be seen as a historical account or as a parable, composed in order to convey a message and perhaps including some elements of midrash (i.e. comment on and development of other passages of Scripture, in this case 2 Kings 14:23–25 in particular). It is often suggested that Jonah is a parable, a form found on several occasions in other Old Testament books. Clearly the book is a brilliant work of art with the emphasis falling on the meaning of the story rather than on the events it narrates. It contains a number of incidents which while they may perhaps not be impossible to explain in historical terms, yet, when taken in conjunction, stretch the imagination to the limit. These include the swallowing of Jonah by the great fish, the immense size of the city as described, the wholesale conversion of the people, and the growth in a single day of the gourd or vine which then withered equally quickly.

Against this view it is urged that Jonah is much longer than any other biblical parable, and that parables do not usually have a real historical figure as their hero. The fact that Jesus uses Jonah as an illustration is perceived as significant (Matthew 12:38–42; Luke 11:29–32). The message of Jonah stands whether the story is a parable or a historical event, and Jesus' reference to the sign of Jonah does not automatically mean that he is taking it for granted that the book of Jonah describes history; he could be referring to Jonah as we might refer to Robin Hood or Superman. However it is very difficult to see how the men of Nineveh could be seen as standing at the judgment to condemn the unbelief of Jesus' own generation if Jonah did not in fact preach to them and they did not in fact respond. One possibility may be that the author of the book of Jonah did have available to him traditions about Jonah's preaching to the Ninevites which he then developed into the book as we have it.

Purpose

Why was the book written? Several answers have been given to this question.

Was it a challenge to missionary endeavour? Jonah is certainly called to a missionary task, even if a somewhat limited one and the book has much to say to those concerned with cross-cultural mission. But there is more concern with Jonah's response to the task than to the task itself and it is difficult to imagine that the book was written as a tract to encourage missionary vision in Israel.

Was it intended to promote universalism, possibly written to counteract the rather narrow exclusivism of the time of Ezra and Nehemiah? Jonah certainly serves to broaden Israel's perspective on the world, but does not deal with the same questions as Ezra and Nehemiah, who were concerned not with Gentiles in general but with the activities of non-Jews in Jerusalem itself.

Was it intended as an explanation of the non-fulfilment of oracles against foreign nations. Prophecy which did not appear to be fulfilled was sometimes a problem for Israel, and by introducing the possibility of God responding to repentance even from foreign nations, Jonah provides an answer. But here again this does not seem to be the main thrust of the story.

Or is it an exploration of the relationship between justice and mercy, similar to that found in Genesis 18–19 where God debates with Abraham about Sodom and Gomorrah?

It is likely that the overall purpose of Jonah is a combination of these and perhaps several other ideas but the main storyline seems to concern the way in which God dealt with one individual and the main teaching points are concerned with the nature of God and the responsibilities of his servants.

SUMMARY OF THE MESSAGE OF JONAH

The Nature of God

God is sovereign over land and sea. Yahweh, the God of Israel, is Lord over all nations, he is much greater than the 'great' city of Nineveh. It is impossible to run away from such a God or ultimately to avoid his purposes.

God will judge the world. He will not tolerate crimes against humanity, and sin which involves a whole nation demands the repentance of that whole nation.

God is supremely compassionate — given the slightest hint of response and repentance he is likely to give the guilty another chance. This basic principle in the experience and faith of Israel is seen here to be equally relevant for other nations.

'Salvation comes from the LORD'. He is presented as the deliverer, of the sailors, of Jonah and of Nineveh. His concerns for people are far broader and far deeper than Jonah had even begun to understand.

God listens to and cares for the individual as well as nations and cities. The book presents him as taking a great deal of trouble to correct Jonah's attitude.

Nationalistic exclusivism is not compatible with God's

character. He has not written off the pagan nations even if they are as corrupt as Assyria; and therefore his people have no right to do so either.

The Responsibilities of the Servant of God

God requires obedience to his commands, even when they seem to go against all the individual's most cherished prejudices.

Knowing the truth is not enough, it must be accepted and applied. Jonah learned that what he believed and proclaimed about God had to be reflected in the way he behaved towards other people.

A servant of God needs to be in sympathy with God's purposes and to reflect God's character. His obedience must be heartfelt and not simply a grudging acceptance because there is no alternative.

JONAH FOR TODAY

The teaching in Jonah is contained largely in the story it tells, which is concerned on the one hand with the reactions of an individual and on the other hand with universal issues. It is perhaps because of the fact that it is not tied down to a particular situation within Israel that the message which the book originally conveyed seems so applicable today.

How many Christians have an element of the Jonah in their character? They may know and believe that God is the God of salvation and feel genuine gratitude for the effects of that in their own lives, but there are certain groups of people who they regard in their heart of hearts as beyond God's reach. Our own particular prejudice may be against catholics or anti-catholics, communists or capitalists, terrorists or white South Africans. Whoever they may be, we cannot believe that they could repent and we are not really sure that they ought to be even given the

Author

The name of Joel's father is given as Pethuel, but nothing
else is known about the prophet. One tradition states that
Joel came from the area of Reuben, but this is almost
certainly based on a misunderstanding of 1 Chronicles 5:4.
Joel appears to have been a fairly common name. The
book shows considerable interest in the fate of Jerusalem
and in particular in temple worship, and a popular suggestion is that Joel was a temple prophet.

Date

The difficulty of accurately fitting Joel into the history of
Israel and Judah is shown by the fact that the same
evidence (the sole source being the book itself), leads
some scholars to date the book well before the exile, as
early as the first half of the eighth century BC, while others
place it long after the exile, as late as the second half of
the fourth century BC. Among the relevant factors are:

a) The nations mentioned as enemies of Judah include
Tyre, Sidon, Philistia, Egypt, Edom and the Greeks.
Notable omissions are Syria, Assyria, Babylon and Persia.
The Greeks were most significant in Judah's history at a
late stage, but this is not conclusive proof of a late date for
Joel, since they were active as early as the eighth century
and the other enemies mentioned were certainly significant
in the era before Assyria and Babylon came on the scene.
However, there is no mention of the northern kingdom of
Israel which seems to indicate a time well after Israel had
been destroyed (722 BC).

b) Although Joel recognizes that cultic ritual can never
replace repentance (2:13), he nevertheless regards it as an
appropriate sign of the people's response and repentance
(1:13–14; 2:15–17). This attitude seems to be very different
from the wholesale condemnation of the cult and its ritual

found in the eighth century prophets (Amos 5:21–23;
Hosea 2:11; Micah 6:6–7; Isaiah 1:11–16 etc.).

c) The book apparently contains many indirect references
to and quotations from the work of other prophets,
including Ezekiel, Amos, and Obadiah. It is always difficult
to say who is citing whom, but the strong indications are
that it is Joel which is secondary. In Joel 2:32, 'as the LORD
has said', specifically identify an earlier oracle (Obadiah
17) and compel us to date Joel after Obadiah.

The evidence is ambiguous, but possibly the balance of
probability places Joel in the fifth century BC after the
return from exile. Fortunately, our understanding of the
teaching of Joel is not limited by uncertainty about dating.
In fact, one of the reasons for the difficulty in dating Joel
is that the book's message is directly relevant to so many
different stages in Judah's history.

Unity

It has been suggested that the original prophecy consisted
simply of the description of the plague of locusts and Joel's
use of this as a warning. The second half, which develops
this into prophecies about the Day of the Lord are, in this
view, a later addition by a different author. However,
there are so many connections between the first half and
the second half, both in language, structure, and concept,
including the day in which God will take action, that most
modern commentators argue strongly that the book should
be seen as a unity.

The use of metaphor

It is not absolutely clear where Joel is speaking metaphori-
cally and where descriptively. Chapter 1 contains an
account of a plague of locusts, and chapter 2 a description

of invading armies couched in similar language but not actually mentioning locusts. The following possibilities arise:

a)   Both chapters are dealing with an actual plague of locusts which Joel interpreted as being sent by God to warn the people of Judah. The plague marked the onset of the process of judgment which would lead to their total destruction unless they responded to the call to repentance. Returning to Yahweh would result in the very different future described in 2:18 – 3:21.

b)   Both chapters are metaphorical and describe an invasion by enemy troops who are being used by God for judgment. If the nation repents then God will take action to restore the material prosperity of the land, and this will also eventually lead to a time of spiritual renewal.

c)   Chapter 1 describes a real plague of locusts which Joel interprets as a warning of an impending enemy invasion which will be totally devastating unless the nation repents.

The Day of the Lord

The concept of the Day of the Lord is central in Joel. The whole book is structured round this picture of the day in which God will act, whether in judgment or in salvation. However, the 'day' in chapter 1 appears to relate to the present time, whereas after 2:28 the reference is apparently to a more distant future. There is thus ambiguity about how far the prophecies relate to the immediate danger of invasion, whether by armies of locusts or of men, and how far they are eschatological, *ie* relating to the last days. Possibly the overlap between these two ideas is deliberate. Was Joel telling his hearers that the God who was acting now would also act decisively in the future? The day of the Lord was not necessarily a single occasion but a process. His actions in the present were to be seen as foreshadowing his actions in the future.

THE MESSAGE OF JOEL

We know very little about the precise situation of those to whom Joel's challenge was originally delivered. He gives no details of specific sins, though he speaks of their 'bloodguilt' (3:21) and challenges them to 'return to me with all your heart' and 'rend your heart and not your garment' (2:12–13). It is clear that they had become complacent and had perhaps substituted religious ritual for genuine obedience and faith. But what seems to have appalled Joel was their general failure to see God's hand in disaster. This wilful blindness, involving civic leaders, priests and people (1:2, 13; 2:1) was a major symptom of their disease. They couldn't — or wouldn't — see that the locusts were in effect God's army. It would take another and more terrible 'day of the LORD' to open their eyes. Joel insists that God is active in their world. Whether this insistence should be seen as a warning or as a statement of hope will depend very much on their reaction and their own relationship with God.

Presuppositions

Joel's understanding of God reflects that of the eighth and seventh century prophets. Some of the presuppositions underlying his oracles are:

God is the Lord of Creation. He is able to use the forces of nature to bring both blessing and judgment (1:1–12; 2:21–24).

God is the righteous Judge of all. He holds all people accountable for their actions and will bring judgment both on Judah and on the nations (1:15; 2:1; 3:2–16).

God is gracious and compassionate. The possibility is always present that, following repentance, judgment will turn into blessing (2:12–14).

God is sovereign and finally, whatever else happens, his name and his people will be honoured (3:17–21).

It is in the context of this understanding of God that Joel warns and reassures his people.

Warnings

To those who do not repent, the vision of the future that Joel presents is terrifying. The people of Judah seem strangely unmoved by the locust plague, but their complacency is far from justified. Both in the short term and in the long term all they can look forward to is disaster on an unprecedented scale (1:2). Whether it comes through locusts or invading armies, it will mean total destruction. Meeting with God will bring no joy and gladness (1:16) rather, 'The day of the Lord is great; it is dreadful. Who can endure it?' (2:11).

However, Joel does not simply warn them to prepare for disaster; he tells them how to avoid it. The form of their disobedience to God is unclear and perhaps irrelevant. Whatever their sin the action needed is the same. They must turn back to God, and worship him in repentance and in faith. However, their worship will at this stage involve weeping, fasting and pleading rather than praise and rejoicing (1:13–14; 2:15–17). He is concerned that their repentance and their faith should be genuine — the ritual signs of this are important but without the right attitudes they are a total waste of time (2:12–14).

Reassurance and Hope

Joel was in no doubt that disaster for Judah was on the way, but equally, he was in no doubt that there would be an 'afterwards' (2:28). After the devastation, God would bring in abundant restoration for the land (2:18–27; 3:17–18) and for the people (2:28–32; 3:20–21). God's Spirit would be made freely available for women and for men, for young and old alike. This salvation was intended for 'all people', yet Joel clearly did not see it as automatic or indeed universal. It would be for 'my servants', that is for 'everyone who calls on the name of the Lord'. For such people the immediate outlook was indeed sad, but the 'day of the LORD' for them would be a time not of terror and despair but of deliverance and hope. An additional reassurance from the perspective of the believing Judeans was the fact that the marauding nations who devastated Judah would themselves come under God's judgment and face destruction.

A TASTER IN JOEL

Joel 2:15–17

Blow the trumpet in Zion,   15
   declare a holy fast,
   call a sacred assembly.
Gather the people,   16
   consecrate the assembly;
bring together the elders,
   gather the children,
   those nursing at the breast.
Let the bridegroom leave his room
   and the bride her chamber.
Let the priests, who minister before the LORD,   17
   weep between the temple porch and the altar.
Let them say, 'Spare your people, O LORD.
   Do not make your inheritance an object of scorn,
   a byword among the nations.
Why should they say among the peoples,
   "Where is their God?"'

The trumpet-call in 2:1 is a signal to mobilize for war. But in these verses it calls the people together for a solemn assembly of prayer and fasting. There has apparently been a genuine, heartfelt turning back to God (12–14). The official ceremony is the formal way of recognizing this. That the call is for a national assembly emphasizes the seriousness of the situation. All have been involved in the sin and all must be brought together to plead with God — even those, like children, nursing mothers and newly married couples, who would normally be excused religious and military duties (Deuteronomy 24:5). The temple priests are to lead the worship, gathering together to weep before God. Joel gives the words of a prayer to be used in this special service. Note that the basis on which they ask God for mercy is not any righteousness or possible worth of their own but the honour and reputation of God himself (cf Ezekiel 36:22–23).

JOEL FOR TODAY

In Acts 2, Peter interprets Joel's prophecy that God's Spirit will be poured out on all people (Joel 2:28–32) as being fulfilled at Pentecost, this understanding of the verses is a tremendous source of encouragement for Christians; it reminds them both that God is working and will continue to work in his church and also that God's plans and purposes have been, and are being, worked out through the centuries. But we should lose a great deal if our involvement with the teaching of Joel were limited to these five verses.

Perhaps because we are unsure about the precise circumstances addressed by Joel and uncertain how far his message refers to contemporary events and how far to the last days, Joel has a timeless relevance. He calls for a whole-hearted response to God's warning voice. Ignoring God when he speaks must lead to disaster when eventually, God acts, as act he will. The terror and devastation Joel evokes when he speaks of judgment are in no way invalidated by New Testament teaching. Similarly, Joel's reassurances that God is loving and gracious, so that those who do survive (2:32) and receive his mercy will experience salvation and great blessing, are only reinforced by an understanding that this mercy is offered by God in Jesus Christ.

The book reminds us that corporate religious life and worship is vitally important — there is a continuing need to come together in prayer. But maintaining religious rituals of any kind can only ever be a means towards attaining our goal of right relationship with God. Joel forces us to ask the question 'Do we take seriously the implications of his teaching about the day of the LORD, that God does act in the present and will act decisively in the future?' The New Testament defines the final 'day of the LORD' as being the day on which Christ returns in glory. Do we view such a prospect with indifference, with fear or with hope and joy?

SECTION III: FURTHER STUDY

QUESTIONS FOR STUDY AND DISCUSSION

1. Show how Nahum illustrates his message of God's sovereignty by reference to the downfall of Nineveh.

2. Are there any situations in today's world where it is right for Christians to pray for and be glad about the downfall of others?

3. Examine Zephaniah's teaching on the 'Day of the Lord'. How does it relate to similar teaching found in the book of Amos?

4. Consider areas in your own life or the life of your church where complacency might have set in. In such a situation, how could the book of Zephaniah be seen as a challenge and an encouragement?

5. 'The book of Habakkuk provides the perfect balance between cynical realism and naive faith'. Discuss.

6. What do you see as the purpose of the book of Habakkuk?

7. Is it true to say that in today's society, and even in today's church, any stress on perseverance in the face of difficulty is seen as unpopular or unacceptable? If you agree, discuss the possible reasons.

8. Write a character study of the prophet Jeremiah.

9. Discuss Jeremiah's understanding of the covenant and of its continuing relevance for Judah.

10. Describe the future for Judah which Jeremiah envisaged.

11. Jeremiah's understanding of what was best for Judah differed from almost all of his fellow Judeans. Can he rightly be described as a patriot?

12. It is often assumed that for the believer, depression implies a lack of faith and a lack of understanding of God's character

and purpose. In the light of Jeremiah's experience assess the accuracy of this assumption.

13. Jeremiah's message of defeat and destruction appeared to contradict the emphasis placed by other religious leaders on God's promises of covenant blessing. Apparently a strong stress on what seems correct doctrine may lead people away from God because it gives only half of the story. Can you think of instances of this happening today?

14. What elements of God's message for the world today might be seen as 'bad news'? Are these elements being proclaimed? By whom?

15. What can we learn from Ohadiah about the right and wrong ways to conduct international relations?

16. Discuss the structure and purpose of the book of Jonah.

17. What does Jonah teach about God and his attitude to the nations?

18. With reference to the book of Jonah, consider the relationship between right behaviour and right motivation.

19. Think about situations in your own life where you have been aware of God's purposes and yet out of sympathy with them. How did you react?

20. Write an introduction to the book of Joel considering the problems of date, authorship, purpose etc.

21. Compare Joel's attitude to ritual cultic worship with that of the eighth century prophets.

22. Joel presents the starkness of the choice facing human beings. They must turn to God, or take the consequences. Does his analysis still apply and if so, how best can such starkness be presented today?

23. Illustrate and discuss the varied use of metaphors, parables and other literary pictures in the pre-exilic prophets.

SUGGESTED FURTHER READING

Allen, L. *The books of Joel, Obadiah, Jonah, Micah* (NICOT) Eerdmans 1976

Baker, D. W. *Nahum, Habakkuk and Zephaniah* (Tyndale OTC) IVP 1988

Baker, D. W., T. D. Alexander & B. K. Waltke *Obadiah, Jonah and Micah* (Tyndale OTC) IVP 1988

Coggins, R. J. & S. E. Re'emi *Nahum, Obadiah and Esther* Eerdmans 1985

Ogden, G. J. & R. R. Deutsch *Joel and Malachi* Eerdmans 1987

R. L. Smith *Micah — Malachi* Word Biblical Commentaries 1984

Stuart, D. *Hosea — Jonah* Word Biblical Commentaries 1987

Watts, J. D. W. *Obadiah* Eerdmans 1969

——*Joel, Obadiah, Jonah, Nahum, Habakkuk and Zephaniah* (Cambridge Bible Commentary) CUP 1975

Wolff, H. W. *Obadiah and Jonah* SPCK 1986

——*Joel and Amos* (Hermeneia) Fortress Press 1977

Bright, J. *Jeremiah* (Anchor Bible) Doubleday 1965

Carroll, R. P. *Jeremiah* (Old Testament Library) SCM 1986

Martens, E. *Jeremiah* Herald Press 1986

Thompson, J. A. *Jeremiah* (NICOT) 1980

SECTION IV

The exile and after

CHAPTER 22

Background: The Exile and After

THE WORLD SITUATION

Babylon remained the major power in the ancient near east for several decades, although none of Nebuchadnezzar's successors were of his stature, and after his death Babylonian influence gradually declined. During the reign of the last king of Babylon, Nabonidus (556–539 BC), Cyrus of Persia was extending his influence. In 550 BC Cyrus took over the Median Empire and adopted an increasingly aggressive policy against Babylon herself, until in 539 BC he conquered the city of Babylon, previously thought to be impregnable. He mounted a surprise attack by diverting the river and entering the city along the dried-up river bed. Belshazzar, Nabonidus' son who had acted as regent, was killed and Nabonidus captured. Cyrus then became emperor, ruling over a massive area, consisting of the whole of western Asia. The evidence seems to indicate that Cyrus was actually welcomed as liberator by the Babylonian people and he certainly proved to be both astute and humane.

Cyrus very quickly introduced a policy of allowing exiled peoples to return to their own lands, taking any confiscated religious treasures with them. There is a well-known Persian chronicle known as the Cyrus cylinder which gives details of the capture of Babylon and the return of the exiles and generally confirms the accuracy of the biblical account (2 Chronicles 36:22 — Ezra 1:8; Isaiah 44:28 – 45:13). Cyrus apparently preferred the nations within the Persian empire to be largely self-governing and he certainly permitted and indeed encouraged them to follow their own religions. Cyrus was replaced eventually by his son Cambyses, on whose death in 522 BC the Median Darius I came to power. He was followed by Xerxes (486–465), Artaxerxes I (465–424), Xerxes II (423), Darius II (423–404) and Artaxerxes II (404–358).

LIFE FOR THE JUDEANS IN EXILE

Once in exile the Judeans were apparently allowed considerable freedom. There was no attempt to absorb them into Babylonian society. They continued to use their own language and as they spread out into surrounding towns and villages formed their own communities led by priests and elders. When Jerusalem was destroyed in 587 BC and the second main group of exiles arrived, those who had been exiled ten years earlier were already settled and ready to welcome them. The early chapters of the book of Daniel give some indication of life at this time, and of the way in which certain gifted young men from amongst the exiles were taken and trained as government administrators for the Babylonians. Further information comes from the book of Ezekiel. Ezekiel himself had been exiled with the first group in 597 BC, and between 592 and 571 BC he acted as a prophet to the exiled community.

Life in the rugged hillsides of Judah had been hard for many years. By contrast, the flatlands of Babylonia, irrigated by a network of canals drawing water from the two great rivers, Tigris and Euphrates, were exceptionally fertile. Farms and small businesses brought prosperity to some of the exiles, and it is perhaps not surprising that when the opportunity was given to return to Judah, many preferred the relative security of their new life-style and refused to go.

BACK IN THE LAND

Yet soon after Cyrus came into power some Jews began to return; presumably including those who had been inspired by the writings of Ezekiel and Isaiah, and had retained their vision for a restored life in their own land. People often think of the return from exile as happening in a very short space of time, but in fact it took place in three stages, over almost a hundred years. There is some debate over the dating, particularly about whether it was Ezra or Nehemiah who arrived in Jerusalem first. However it seems very likely that the main party returned in 538/7 BC with Zerubbabel. This group immediately built an altar and probably laid the foundations for the temple, but the temple itself was not finished until approximately twenty years later in 516 BC. A second group, led by Ezra, went back in 458 BC, some sixty years after the temple was rebuilt, and the last group in 445 BC with Nehemiah.

Thus it took many years to re-establish and re-build the nation. We are given details of these years in the books of Ezra and Nehemiah. It may have been only a remnant who returned, but they arrived home in triumph, filled with enthusiasm, supported by the blessing of the emperor and with much financial help from those who did not want to return with them. It had seemed impossible, but the prophetic predictions had come to pass. The figure of forty-two thousand mentioned in Ezra 2:64 probably refers to those returning on several occasions and not just to the first group, but the first group was by far the largest. Sheshbazzar was appointed governor and the returned exiles began to settle in. They made a good start; the land was badly neglected but they settled down to put it to rights. After seven months, Zerubbabel, a descendant of David who later took over from Sheshbazzar as leader of the community, rebuilt the altar. Regular sacrifices could now be offered once again. The people began to organize supplies for re-building the temple itself and five months later the foundations were laid (Ezra 2:70 – 3:13).

However, after that things began to go wrong and the

next few years proved very disappointing. The land was in a much worse state than they had expected; the local residents, some few left behind at the exile and others who had moved in since, were not glad to see them; and neighbouring provinces who saw the new state as a threat did all they could to prevent the community from getting established. To make things even worse, there were several years of very poor harvests. Depression set in and over the next eighteen years virtually nothing was done. However, in 520 BC, two new prophets, Haggai and Zechariah, started speaking out. They brought new inspiration to the disheartened community, and encouraged by these prophets, the community completed the rebuilding of the temple.

We are told very little of events in the Jewish community over the next sixty years. The earlier hopes for complete independence and a restored Davidic monarchy remained unfulfilled. But the community did survive and when Ezra and Nehemiah arrived to give new enthusiasm and encouragement, it was strong enough to make a very positive response. We do not have an exact date for Malachi, the last of the Old Testament prophets. His ministry took place after 520 BC when the temple was rebuilt, either just before, or just after, the work of Nehemiah, many of whose concerns he shared.

CHAPTER 23

Ezekiel

EZEKIEL — THE MAN

His Life and Background

Ezekiel, the son of Buzi, was born and brought up in or around Jerusalem but he was deported and taken into exile in Babylon, almost certainly with the group accompanying Jehoiachin in 597 BC (2 Kings 24:14–17). From then on, he lived at Tel-Abib by the River Kebar. Like Jeremiah he came from a priestly family and it seems clear that he himself was being trained as a priest. He certainly shows a detailed knowledge of Jerusalem and of the cultic rules and his writing is strongly influenced by priestly symbolism. However his ministry was in no way restricted by priestly legalism or formalism. He also shows a good knowledge of the writing prophets, and although he never mentions him by name, was almost certainly aware of Jeremiah and his work. But one of the greatest influences on his life and ministry, which apparently changed his own thinking quite radically, was the vision of God which he received at his call.

After spending five years in exile he experienced a call to be a prophet, probably at the age of 30, the time when under normal circumstances he would have commenced his official priestly duties. 1:1 is not absolutely clear, but this would have been a very significant time for Ezekiel and it is difficult to know what the 'thirtieth year' refers to, if it is not to Ezekiel's age. If he was 30 at this time, then he would have been a teenager when Josiah died and would have been aware of the reforms and also of the lack of real response to them.

After his initial vision, he worked amongst the exiles as a prophet during the five years up to the fall of Jerusalem and for at least a further seventeen years after that. The latest date mentioned in the book is the twenty-seventh year of exile (29:17, 571 BC) and there is no reference to subsequent events. There is a minor dating problem in 33:21, which says that the news of the fall of Jerusalem arrived towards the end of the twelfth year of exile. This should almost certainly read 'in the eleventh year', because it is extremely unlikely that the message would have taken eighteen months to get through.

Chapters 8–11 describe a vision in which Ezekiel was transported to Jerusalem and saw and spoke to the people there. It was at one time suggested that these chapters describe what actually happened in a period of ministry in Jerusalem prior to his exile. However, if this was so, it is difficult to understand why the text should so clearly present it as a vision given in exile. The oracles relating to foreign nations contain several examples of messages apparently directed to one group of people actually being intended for another (25:1 – 32:32), and the detailed knowledge of Jerusalem revealed here could easily have come from previous experience, from further information received in letters and from his own spiritual insight.

Within the exiled community there appears to have been a great deal of freedom; both for individuals to travel and for the community to organize itself. Ezekiel appears to have held a position of respect among the exiles, although whether because of his prophetic role or because of the status of his family is not clear. Certainly he was regularly visited by the community elders (8:1; 14:1; 20:1). However, although he was listened to, in general his message was not well received or heeded (3:25; 33:30–32).

Of Ezekiel's personal life we know little. He had a

number of visionary experiences; there were times when
for some reason he was unable to move or speak; he used
a number of somewhat bizarre actions to illustrate his
message; he was happily married to a wife he loved; but
when she died he was required, also in order to illustrate
his message, not to show public signs of mourning (24:15–
27). On the one hand, Ezekiel appears as a formal,
pedantic legal and cultic expert, a hard-line denouncer.
On the other hand, we find a mystical visionary, a loving
husband and a caring pastor. To understand the book of
Ezekiel we must have some appreciation of these different
sides to his nature.

Ezekiel's Commission

We do not know what kind of person Ezekiel was before,
in the great vision beside the Kebar River, he came face to
face with the glory of God. Perhaps he agreed with those
of the exiles who were convinced that Jehoiachin would
return to Jerusalem and the kingdom be restored. He may
have experienced the despair of those who felt that they
were abandoned by God, condemned for the sins of their
ancestors and unable to do anything about their plight.
Perhaps he shared the sense of isolation of those first
exiles who thought that God's purposes still lay with those
who had remained in Jerusalem and that the exiles could
have no share in it — with the added frustration of
knowing he could not take up his vocation as a priest.
Certainly Ezekiel was aware of all these groups and much
of his prophecy is concerned with answering their problems and misunderstandings. But the force that drove
Ezekiel, that gave focus to all his oracles and kept him
going in the face of opposition, indifference and mockery
was the overwhelming awareness of God's holiness that
had come to him through his vision.

His own call to be a prophet came in the context of this
experience of the glory of God. As the Israelites understood
the matter, this glory had been centred on the temple at

Jerusalem; but after his vision Ezekiel knew, without a shadow of a doubt, that it could also be experienced, in all its fulness, elsewhere, even in exile. He saw and tried to express in inadequate human words his vision of God as 'unutterably splendid, mysteriously intricate, super-human and supernatural, infinitely mobile but never earth-bound, all-seeing and all-knowing' (J. B. Taylor *Ezekiel* IVP p. 41). He was also convinced of the vital importance of people knowing who this God was. Variations of the phrase 'and they/you/the nations will know that I am Yahweh (the Lord)' are found more than seventy-five times in the first thirty-nine chapters of Ezekiel.

The account of Ezekiel's call in 2:1 – 3:15 does not actually say what his message was to be, but he is told to deliver it to a 'rebellious nation' who would not be at all willing to listen to him. Ezekiel is always addressed by God as 'son of man', a title which probably has nothing to do with the expression as used in Daniel 7:13, but which is used to emphasize the human weakness of Ezekiel over against the sovereign holiness of God whose message Ezekiel proclaims. He was very aware both of the heaviness of his own responsibility as a watchman (3:16–27; 33:1–20) sent to warn the people of danger, and also of the fact that more often than not they saw him as a popular entertainer, rather like a pop-singer, enjoyable to listen to, but with no need to take any notice of the words (33:30–33).

At his commissioning, Ezekiel realized he was being sent to God's stubborn, rebellious people to destroy any hope that the regime in Jerusalem might be restored and to convince the exiles that God's judgment would be followed through to the bitter end. But he did not perceive God as unfaithful to his promises, unjust or impotent. Later on Ezekiel proclaimed a message of hope, but not until the lessons of judgment had been fully learned. At that point Ezekiel's role changed and he had the task of encouraging the development of a new community who would want to love and serve God and who would properly represent God's interests.

EZEKIEL — THE BOOK

Unlike Jeremiah, Ezekiel is a well-structured book, arranged according to clearly discernible principles. There are four major sections. Chapters 1–24 contain prophecies given before the fall of Jerusalem. Here Ezekiel speaks in no uncertain terms of the people's sin and the futility of hoping that Jerusalem would be saved from destruction. Chapters 25–32 form an intermediate section containing oracles against foreign nations. Chapters 33–39 move on from the fall of Jerusalem and begin to look to the future, speaking of eventual return from exile and a new start. Chapters 40–48 contain a vision of the new temple and make extensive use of symbolic and metaphorical language.

Fourteen of the sub-sections are given a precise date and it is clear that in general the material is arranged chronologically. The exception to this is the second section, in which the oracles dealing with foreign nations have been collected together and used to separate the prophecies of judgment from those of hope. Within this generally chronological framework we find a number of thematic sections. Thus chapters 12–14 contain four prophecies about prophets and prophecy, and chapters 15–19 are all allegories, parables or discussion of proverbs.

In some respects, the book is uniform. The style and the language used remain very similar throughout, and the whole is written in the first person without any sign of the third person narratives found in many of the other prophetic books. However it is made clear that the prophecies were all given at different times and it is apparent that a great deal of editorial activity has taken place in bringing it all together. Until the beginning of this century it was taken for granted that the book had been produced in its entirety by Ezekiel himself. But then a number of scholars began to question this assumption, and it was even suggested that as much as eighty per cent of the material was added by a group of Ezekiel's disciples. This extreme view has been rejected and Ezekiel's part in the book as a

whole is widely recognized, although the possibility of an
external editor is not discounted and some would suggest
that chapters 40–48 were written by a different hand. Any
editing, whether by Ezekiel himself or somebody else,
must have taken place fairly soon after the final prophecies
in 571 BC. Certainly the book shows no awareness of
events after the time of Nebuchadnezzar.

Ezekiel's style of writing is somewhat ponderous and
stilted; this and the use of stereotyped phrases makes the
book rather difficult to read. Yet, Ezekiel's own enthusiasm
and fervour does come across through this rather heavy
style and there is some variety in the material.

Four sections, (1:1 – 3:15; 8 – 11; 37; 40–48) describe
visionary experiences in which messages were given to
Ezekiel when he was in an ecstatic or trance state. It is
irrelevant to ask whether these visions involved actual
experiences or took place in Ezekiel's mind. In either case,
they had a profound effect on him and he recorded them
so that they might also affect his readers. The book
includes descriptions of symbolic actions (4:1–3, 9–12; 5:1–4;
12:3–6, 18; 21:19–20; 24:16–17; 37:16–17), laments, and dis-
cussions of the value of certain proverbs and allegories, as
well as more straightforward prophecies of judgment and
of restoration.

OUTLINE

1:1 – 24:27 Before the fall of Jerusalem : mainly judgment

13:1 – 14:23 Condemnation of false prophets and idolaters
15:1 – 17:23 Pictures of Jerusalem — her unfaithfulness
          and God's action
18:1–32   Responsibility of the individual — a case history
19:1–14   Lament for Israel
20:1 – 24:27 Israel's rebellion and God's use of Babylon to
          punish her

25:1 – 32:32 Prophecies against the nations

33:1 – 39:29 After the fall of Jerusalem — hope for the future

33:1–20   Ezekiel the watchman
33:21–33   News of Jerusalem's defeat
34:1–31   Israel's leaders as cruel, greedy shepherds.
          God as the Good Shepherd
35:1–15   Edom's treachery will be repaid
36:1 – 37:28 Prophecies of new life for Israel's dry bones
38:1 – 39:20 A prophecy against Gog
39:21–29   God's purposes for Israel

40:1 – 48:35 The New Jerusalem

40:1 – 42:20 Vision of the new temple
43:1–12   God's glory returns to the temple
43:13 –   Temple organization and arrangements for
46:24   worship
47:1–12   The life-giving river flows from the temple
47:13 –   The division of the land and the gates of the
48:35   city

THE MESSAGE OF EZEKIEL

The message of Ezekiel could be summarized very briefly.
'Because of Israel's sin (Although he is speaking to Judah,

he refers to the nation as "Israel"), God will destroy Jerusalem and bring to an end the life that Israel had previously known in the land. Subsequently, concern for his own honour, will lead God to take a group from among the exiles and restore them to new life back in their own land'.

However, the details of this message deserve much closer attention.

The Holy God — His Nature

Ezekiel's vibrant personal awareness of the God with whom he and his people have to deal comes across throughout the book. In particular he speaks of God's glorious and awesome holiness. Through his visions, Ezekiel learned that God's greatness and purity surpassed anything that Israel had ever realized (1:25–28; 3:23; 5:11; 36:23). It was this experience that gave Ezekiel the freedom to speak out against those who reiterated traditional beliefs, such as that God would never allow his temple to be destroyed. Ezekiel realized that the traditions must be subjected to God and not vice versa. The power of this holy God extended to every place (3:12–27; 5:5) and he was supreme over all peoples (25:1–32:32). His glory was as real in Babylon as in Jerusalem.

The sense of God's freedom not to be bound by their limited understanding of him comes across very strongly in the vision of God's glory actually departing from the temple (9:3–11:23). That this should happen made it impossible for anybody still to think that God did not care about sin. The further description of God's glory returning (43:1–5), not because they in any sense deserved it, but just because it was the way God chose to proclaim his own honour, answered the doubters who suggested that God was not able to save. In the first twenty-four chapters, Ezekiel portrays God as an unbending judge who will carry out his judgment but this is by no means the only aspect of God's character that Ezekiel knew and proclaimed.

He is absolutely just (18:25; 33:20), he is the loving Lord, who is deeply involved with his people and who guides and directs them (2:2; 11:1,5). He cares for them like a good shepherd (34:11–16), and even though there is no life left in them, he will take the dry bones that remain and bring restoration and renewal (36:25 – 37:28).

Part of the tension in Ezekiel's ministry came from his conviction that new life could only come through death. The people knew Yahweh as the God of Israel and Judah. In one sense it was only their links with Jerusalem and the community still there that held the exiles together as Yahweh worshippers. Yet Ezekiel knew that those ties must be completely severed so that a new relationship with Yahweh could be worked out. Prophets like Ezekiel and Jeremiah prophesied the fall of the nation, with the loss of Jerusalem and of the land God had given them. But this was not a blasphemous denial of God's power, it involved a recognition of God as he really is.

The Seriousness of Israel's Sin

Ezekiel's message of punishment, judgment and destruction seems at first sight to be cruel and unfeeling. The people were in exile, disheartened and discouraged. Surely they needed comfort and help, not fierce criticism? But there could be no hope for the future that ignored the facts of the past. It was vital that the people recognized the significance of the exile as a punishment and were shamed into real repentance. As Ezekiel pointed out, both the people who had remained in Jerusalem and those who had first been taken into exile were rotten to the core. Neither group could or should be viewed as a righteous remnant (such as Isaiah had described). They had defiled the very temple that they thought would protect them (5:11; 23:38). They were idolaters and even practised child sacrifice (20:7, 18, 26, 31; 22:4). The description of their idolatry in chapter 16 uses very strong language; it is offensive, and intentionally so. The people had ignored the requirements of the law, both ritual (44:6–8) and moral (22:7,12) and yet had thought that this would not affect God's support for them.

For Ezekiel there was no question that they deserved all that was coming to them. God's justice meant that the punishment must be carried out; only his great patience had delayed it so long. But now God's patience had at last run out. The judgment which could neither be ignored or avoided, was coming not as other prophets had foretold, 'on that (future) day' but 'now' (7:10–27; 12:22,27; 22:14; 24:14).

The God of Action — in the Present and the Future

The God of Israel was a God of action. As Ezekiel stresses time and time again, Yahweh wanted to be 'known' by human beings, particularly by his own people but also by foreign nations. In general it was through his deeds that God could be known; by them God's honour would not only be vindicated but be seen to be vindicated. In the years leading up to the fall of Jerusalem, those deeds involved punishment and destruction. By his actions, Yahweh would make it clear that he would not tolerate evil and disobedience. Israel had thought that the honour of God and the honour of Israel were identical. The truth was that Israel herself had dishonoured God's name, prompting God to act in judgment in order to preserve his own honour. Once Jerusalem had fallen and God's honour had been vindicated in judgment, Ezekiel could begin to speak of the way in which God, again acting for the sake of his own glory, would bring new life to his people.

This new life was available to those exiles who accepted the challenge to repent and, in faith, join God's new community. God was offering them this opportunity, not because of any supposed obligation arising out of the old covenant, but out of his great grace (36:16–32). In words very reminiscent of Jeremiah's description of the new covenant (Jeremiah 31), Ezekiel spoke of God giving them a new living heart and a new living spirit to replace their existing hearts of stone (11:19; 36:26). Although this inward renewal would be God's gift, it would also involve their own will and commitment. Repentance was a condition of receiving the new heart (18:31).

Ezekiel envisaged the new community as united; Israel and Judah would be re-joined (37:15–17). They would be joined also to God in an eternal covenant relationship (14:11; 37:23). They would be led by the true shepherd, described both as God himself and as a Davidic messiah-king (34:11,23; 37:24–28). Through them, new life would be brought to the whole world (47:1–12).

When Ezekiel describes how God will act in the future, it is not always clear how far he is referring to the future immediately following the return from exile and how far he is speaking in eschatological terms, referring to the end times. Certainly the vision described in chapters 40–48 was recognized as eschatological, even by the returned exiles. There was never any attempt to use it as a blueprint for rebuilding the community in Jerusalem. However it is worth pointing out that the book does not make any clear distinction between the immediate and the distant future, between the temporal and the eternal. Perhaps we should resist the temptation to introduce a rigorous separation of the two ideas. What is clear is that for the people of Israel, the exile is not to be the end. God still has plans for the future and his purpose includes them. When God's work is finished, then he will have a people who will be like him and who will be able to represent him in the world.

The Characteristics and Responsibilities of God's Servants

Ezekiel's purpose went beyond conveying information about what God would do. He had a genuine concern for the exiles. For their own sake he wanted them both to understand the reality of God's judgment and to experience the great encouragement offered by his message of hope. He also answered the question of what should be done in their immediate situation. He took their problems and questions seriously and answered them carefully, although not always giving the answers they wanted or expected (14:1–23; 18:1–32). He presented them with a way forward; they should wait for God to act in redemption and in the meantime live their lives in a way befitting those who were in community with Yahweh. The characteristics of righteous persons are summarized in chapter 18; they follow God's guidance and sincerely commit themselves to God, their lives are directed towards pleasing God, they know and trust in God's care for them, they are marked out by the wholesomeness of their life-style, known for their purity, obedience to God and for concern shown to others.

Ezekiel presents the responsibilities of the individual very clearly (18:1–32; 33:7–20). Every person is responsible before God for what they do. Neither family background nor present circumstances can in the end be blamed for the way a person turns out. Even one's own past actions are not to be seen as determinative for the future. Each individual must make a choice as to whether or not he or she will serve God and keep on serving God, whose greatest desire is that they should repent, turn to him and receive forgiveness and new life. Ezekiel was certainly aware that there was a corporate national responsibility, and that a person's fate was tied up with the behaviour of his forebears. The exile itself was evidence of that. But this could never be the whole story and when he was confronted by the sort of fatalism which assumes that one's own behaviour is irrelevant, because the future is already determined by factors outside one's own control, he opposed it uncompromisingly.

Ezekiel's teaching about responsibility was strongly influenced by his own sense of his own responsibility as a prophet. He had been called to be a watchman, or a look-out (3:12–21; 33:1–9). He knew that God would hold him to account for any who might perish because of his failure to warn of God's impending judgment. He was particularly scathing about those prophets and other leaders in Israel who failed to take their responsibilities seriously (11:1–15; 13:1–23; 34:1–19). Leaders should depend on God totally and obey him implicitly. They should be dedicated to their task and not afraid to speak out. They should identify themselves with the people they lead, caring for them and being aware of their needs. They should make decisions based on truth and justice and not on self-interest or love of comfort. False prophecies of encouragement based on a false dependence on or a false understanding of God's promises could do untold harm by inducing a false complacency and a wrong picture of God. Ezekiel picks up and develops Jeremiah's denunciation of such prophets in 13:10–12 (c.f. Jeremiah 28:8–9; 29:8–9).

TASTERS IN EZEKIEL

1. *Ezekiel 18:1–4*

The word of the LORD came to me:
'What do you people mean by quoting this proverb   2
   about the land of Israel:

  ' "The fathers eat sour grapes,
  and the children's teeth are set on edge"?

'As surely as I live, declares the Sovereign   3
   LORD, you will no longer quote this proverb in Israel.
For every living soul belongs to me, the father as   4
   well as the son—both alike belong to me. The soul
   who sins is the one who will die.'

These verses are the introduction to an extended discussion of personal responsibility. The discussion deals, in particular, with the effect on responsibility and accountability of the relationship between father and son, but the chapter makes it clear that what is said is meant to be seen as relating to the whole of Israel. Ezekiel picks up a proverb (quoted also in Jeremiah 31:29) and shows how, although generally accepted as true, it actually misrepresents reality.

Similar passages based on different proverbs are found in 12:21–25 and 33:23–29.

According to the proverb, the bitter taste in the mouths of the 'children' was a consequence of what the 'fathers' had eaten. If the people were exiled because of the cumulative sins of previous generations then the application of the proverb is obvious. It was possibly being quoted as a complaint against God, suggesting that he had not been fair to them (cf. v25), or simply as an excuse for ignoring the prophet's message. The feeling was, 'it's not my fault, so I can't be expected to do anything about it'. In response, Ezekiel does not offer a reasoned argument. He merely asserts that the proverb is wrong and will be shown to be wrong, therefore it will fall into disuse. To the extent that this attitude misrepresents God, it could even be seen as blasphemous which possibly accounts for the use of the divine oath, 'As surely as I live', in v3.

Verse 4 is notable because of God's affirmation that each person is important to him as an individual and that each will be judged according to what he or she personally is and does. It is not true that God is concerned only with the nation as a whole — though Ezekiel says elsewhere that he is concerned with that too. Implicit in the claim that 'every living soul belongs to me' is God's sovereign freedom to deal with each person as he pleases.

We need to bear in mind that this is not a theological treatise, but a prophetic message to a particular group of people operating under a particular misunderstanding. It does not present the total picture of God's dealings with men, and it would be foolish to accuse Ezekiel of inconsistency because elsewhere he presupposes a common national destiny.

The complaining attitude of the exiles shown here may reflect the feeling that, although they had been told that they were the 'remnant', it appeared to them unjust that those left behind in Jerusalem still seemed to be better off. This may explain why the proverb is described as being 'about the land of Israel'.

2. *Ezekiel 34:1-6*

The word of the LORD came to me:
'Son of man, prophesy against the shepherds of 2
Israel; prophesy and say to them: "This is what the
Sovereign LORD says: Woe to the shepherds of Israel
who only take care of themselves! Should not
shepherds take care of the flock?
You eat the curds, clothe yourselves with the wool 3
and slaughter the choice animals, but you do not
take care of the flock.
You have not strengthened the weak or healed the 4
sick or bound up the injured. You have not brought
back the strays or searched for the lost. You have
ruled them harshly and brutally.
So they were scattered because there was no 5
shepherd, and when they were scattered they
became food for all the wild animals.
My sheep wandered over the mountains and on 6
every high hill. They were scattered over the whole
earth, and no-one searched or looked for them."'

This chapter contains two units linked by the theme of
sheep. Verses 1–16 tell of the judgment on wicked shepherds and their replacement by Yahweh himself. Verses
17–31 distinguish between good and bad sheep and speak
of a new Davidic shepherd.

Verses 1–6 use the imagery of shepherding to depict the
behaviour of the contemporary leaders of Israel. The term
shepherd was often used to describe rulers in Israel,
especially by Jeremiah (Jeremiah 3:15; 10:21; 50:6). It
was also used outside Israel, for example in the Code of
Hammurabi. It is sometimes suggested that its use should
be restricted to kings, but the application is likely to be
wider. In any case, it was in common usage and people
would have easily understood what was expected of an
ideal shepherd.

In denouncing the shepherds of Israel, Ezekiel contrasts

the way they should have been behaving with their actual conduct. It parallels another prophetic condemnation (Jeremiah 23:1–4) but is more specific. Verse 3 accuses the leaders of exploiting the privileges associated with being shepherds but ignoring the responsibilities. In such a context, as in most others, rights without responsibilities lead to injustice. (NIV is right to translate the term for 'fat' here as 'curds' or milk fat. The shepherds are not being condemned for eating meat fat, forbidden by the ritual law.) Verse 4 lists the responsibilities they have neglected and gives an interesting insight into Ezekiel's concept of ideal leadership, seen here in terms of caring rather than ruling, with gentleness predominant rather than force. In verse 4 the emphasis is on helping those who have been hurt; in verses 5–6 it is more, as it were, on prevention, combating the risk of injury. Both elements are important in Ezekiel's view of leadership. The mention of 'scattering' may be perceived as blaming the rulers for the exile, but may equally refer to the dispersion in general or even to the spiritually 'lost' state of the community.

3.　*Ezekiel 36:22–23,32*

'Therefore say to the house of Israel, ''This is　　　　22
　　what the Sovereign LORD says: It is not for your
　　sake, O house of Israel, that I am going to do these
　　things, but for the sake of my holy name, which you
　　have profaned among the nations where you
　　have gone.
I will show the holiness of my great name, which　　　23
　　has been profaned among the nations, the name
　　you have profaned among them. Then the nations
　　will know that I am the LORD, declares the
　　Sovereign LORD, when I show myself holy
　　through you before their eyes. . .

I want you to know that I am not doing this for　　　32
　　your sake, declares the Sovereign LORD. Be

ashamed and disgraced for your conduct, O house
of Israel!"'

These verses emphasize the basis of God's action. This
concept sandwiches the section on the purposes which
God has for Israel and the action he will take on her
behalf.

Because Yahweh is who he is, he must be truly represented by his actions. The fundamental reason for his saving
activity is to be found in the nature of God and is, in this
instance, not based on mercy, love, or even covenant. This
does not belittle or deny God's love for the people, rather
it emphasizes the fact that Israel as the one who is loved,
does not exercise control over the one who loves. There is
nothing in Israel that should give them any cause for
pride. In one sense even the return from exile should only
make them ashamed rather than jubilant, because it emphasized their own unworthiness (v32). One of the main
purposes of the exile was to deliver them from the self-
righteous pride that was the major cause of their trouble.
There is no way, therefore that the return from exile
should be seen as a cause for pride.

Note that it is not because God is hard or unfeeling that
he insists on the vindication of his honour. Rather it is
because, if humanity is to have any hope at all it must be
based on an accurate realization of who God is; his
holiness, his righteousness, his total sovereignty. Without
such an understanding of the true nature of God, worship
will degenerate into idolatry.

EZEKIEL FOR TODAY

Ezekiel is not always easy for modern readers to appreciate
or understand. One reason for this is the style, another is
the unfamiliar imagery he uses, particularly when describing his visions. It is worth noting that early readers also
found it difficult. Some rabbis in the first century AD tried
to get Ezekiel withdrawn from public use and to prevent

even trainee rabbis from reading certain sections until they
reached the age of 30. There are three possible reasons for
this: the explicit language used in passages like chapter 16;
the mystic language used in chapters 1–2, which could
cause younger readers to become more concerned with
these challenging and attractive mysteries than with hearing and obeying God; and the fact that the buildings and
ritual described in chapters 40–48 differ on some points
from the Mosaic Law and could therefore be seen as
contradicting it. Admittedly, Ezekiel makes full use of
metaphor and other forms of symbolic imagery and it
would be wrong to impose a literalistic interpretation on
sections where such imagery is used. However, readers of
the Bible lose a great deal if because of some initial
difficulties they miss out on the message and on the
relevance of the book of Ezekiel.

Ezekiel is particularly helpful in reminding those who
profess allegiance to the God of the Bible that he is not to
be trifled with or taken for granted, and that attempts to
try and manipulate God are ludicrous. For us, as for
Ezekiel, God is still the Holy One, still infinitely greater
than anything we can imagine, totally pure and totally
just. He still requires wholehearted allegiance and does
not tolerate hypocrisy or misrepresentation. Is the God we
worship God as he has shown himself to be, or is he some
distortion arising from our own imagination? God revealed
himself to Ezekiel as the awesome, glorious one who
demands complete obedience and who will bring judgment on all who deserve it. No less is he the one who
wants everybody to know who he is and what he is like
and who longs for people to be saved. By nature he is the
kind and loving shepherd who binds up the wounds of
straying sheep and restores them to the pasture where
they belong. He still takes bones which are as dry as dust
and transforms them into living men and women.

Ezekiel also reminds us, in a unique way, of what God
expects from his people today in terms of personal responsibility. We, like Israel, will be held responsible for
what we do with our lives and with the opportunities

which God has given to us. Christians also need to ask whether there is anything in their behaviour, as individuals, as churches, or as the whole Christian community, that dishonours God's name. It is easy to look at historical episodes such as the Inquisition or the Holocaust and recognize the disastrous mistakes made by those who called themselves Christians. But we can easily be blind to present day phenomena which are often seen by outsiders as characterizing the church today. Blindness to the needs of the Third World, internal divisions, lack of concern for the poor, seeking status or financial gain, patronizing attitudes towards newer churches — these surely dishonour God. Again like Israel, we need to beware of easy dependence on promises of 'Peace' from religious leaders (13:10), and to recognize the danger of seeking messages from God without first removing the 'idols' to which we have devoted ourselves (14:1–11). Our relationship with God cannot be divorced from our day to day lives.

In a remarkable way, Ezekiel foreshadows the New Testament teaching on leadership as serving rather than ruling. It is very tempting to concentrate on the status or the privileges that are often associated with leadership and thus lose sight of the task. Those who take on positions of leadership of any kind must be aware of their responsibilities. They cannot evade some accountability for those in their care. When individuals fall by the wayside because they have not been warned of dangers, then leaders share the blame. If members of the 'flock' are in pain or damaged, leaders are responsible to help, to heal and to do what they can to prevent further damage. Certainly a leader must sometimes exercise authority and even discipline, but it is important that motives are examined. If I am a leader and my major concerns are to bully the people into doing what I want, to push them beyond their limits, or to rebuke them for not giving me the respect I feel I deserve then my understanding of leadership needs to be corrected by what Ezekiel has to say.

We can also benefit from Ezekiel's perspective on the

future. There is little to be gained by poring over his
visions, working out detailed schemes describing exactly
what God is going to do in the future, or building scale
models of the temple he pictures. But we, no less than
Ezekiel, need to recognize that the God who has acted in
the past will also act in the future, and that because he is
who he is, that action will be both glorious and victorious.
Ezekiel's horrified contemporaries opposed the prophet
when he pictured God's glory departing from Israel and
leaving the temple. But he affirmed that defeat would not
be the final answer, that the time would come when God's
glory would return to a new temple, where the presence
of the living would be a source of life to all. Christians
who have the additional insight that the New Testament
provides, can be even more confident about the final
victory and the coming of God's kingdom. Do we allow
that encouragement an active role in shaping our outlook
on life?

Haggai

OUTLINE

HISTORICAL AND LITERARY CONSIDERATIONS

Background

Cyrus the Persian, after conquering the Medes in 550 BC, then went on to take power in Babylon itself in 539 BC. He immediately issued an edict enabling communities who had been exiled to return to their own land. In 538 BC a group of exiles returned to Jerusalem with the intention of repopulating the land, rebuilding the temple and re-establishing the life of the nation there. But when they returned they were discouraged by the difficulties they experienced. There were too few people to do all that needed doing; the devastation in the city and the surrounding countryside was worse than they had expected; neighbouring tribes were very hostile; and there was a series of poor harvests. It is not surprising that the initial enthusiasm of the return, which had resulted in the altar being re-built and the foundations of the temple being laid, soon disappeared.

The first leaders of the new community were Sheshbazzar (Ezra 1:8–11), Zerubbabel, a descendant of David (Ezra 2:2; 3:2; Haggai 1:1), and Joshua the high priest (Ezra 2:2; 3:2; Haggai 1:1). Zerubbabel was Jehoiachin's grandson (1 Chronicles 3:17) but we cannot be certain of the exact relationship between Sheshbazzar and Zerubbabel, nor of the precise part played by each of these men. It appears that both Haggai and Zechariah thought that Zerubbabel might be the promised Messiah (Haggai 2:23; Zechariah 4:14) but these hopes were not fulfilled and after the time of these prophets, we hear no more of Zerubbabel. Perhaps exaggerated claims were made for him and the Persian authorities took steps to repress a possible source of opposition. Certainly no royal successor was appointed and the leadership of the community appears to have been in the hands of the high priests until the appointment of Nehemiah in the following century.

We know of no prophetic activity in these early years until 520 BC, when, a little over a year after Darius I took over as emperor, Haggai and Zechariah both began to speak out. It may be that during the reign of Cambyses, who preceded Darius, there were difficulties about exercising a prophetic ministry. It was eighteen years after the original return when Haggai did speak out and challenged the leaders and the people to fulfil their commission and complete rebuilding the temple. There is no mention of major moral problems within the community or of great irreligion, the accusation is simply that they had failed to give the building of the temple the priority it should have had.

Authorship

Haggai is described as 'the prophet' in his own book and

in Ezra but we have no further details or aids to identification. This may indicate that he was well known and no further identification was necessary. It may imply the rarity of prophets at that time — schools of prophets were apparently no longer in existence. A number of suggestions are made. One is that Haggai was born in Jerusalem and had seen the original temple for himself (2:3), before being taken into exile. He was now, therefore, a very old man and possibly died soon after his period of prophetic activity. A variation on this view is that he had lived the whole time in Judaea. Another suggestion is that he had been born in exile and been brought to Jerusalem with the return party as a child. This would explain why his name does not occur in any of the lists in Ezra. The name Haggai derives from the word for a feast, and it may be that he was born on the day of a festival.

We can only speculate on these matters. We do not know whether Haggai worked as a prophet before or after this time, but we do know that during a period of just fifteen weeks in the year 520 BC, Haggai gave four separate oracles relating to the effect that completing or not completing the temple building would have on the future of the community. Unlike the messages of many of his predecessors, Haggai's words fell on receptive ears. Work on the temple quickly recommenced and by 516 BC it was completed.

In the book of Haggai we have a summary of these four oracles placed in an editorial framework. Haggai is referred to in the third person and although it is possible that Haggai himself chose to record his words in this way, it seems more likely that they were collected and recorded by somebody else. The book was almost certainly compiled soon after the oracles were delivered, still during the reign of Darius I and before Zerubbabel had dropped out of the picture. The author may even have had access to Haggai's own notes. A less likely suggestion is that the messages were preserved orally and written up some hundred or more years later to restress Haggai's message of the need for wholehearted dedication to God as the first priority in the life of the community.

THE MESSAGE OF HAGGAI

From the outline of Haggai we see that the book is organized into a two-fold structure. The first cycle of challenge, response and promise in effect looks backward, asking what has happened to give rise to the present situation. Haggai, very conscious that he is speaking as God's representative, states that the reason life has been so difficult for the community is the low priority they have given to the task of re-building the temple. Then, because they respond positively to this challenge, he describes how God will bring new glory to the new temple.

In the second cycle, he issues a new challenge about the way things are to be done in the future and finally delivers a promise concerning God's future work through Zerubbabel. The teaching of Haggai's 38 verses can be summarized under three headings.

Teaching about God

Haggai was convinced that God had things to say to the people and that the messages he brought to them came directly from God. Almost thirty times in the two chapters we are told that it is God's word being spoken. This emphasizes both God's involvement with them, and the fact that the prophet was not speaking without authority. God is all-powerful. He is able to 'shake' the universe and the nations (2:6–8; 21–22). He is in control of creation so that Haggai perceived the poor harvests as a sign of God's judgment. If the community would give God first place, then he would shower them with material blessing. God's involvement with them extended to influencing their response, 'stirring up' the hearts of the people (1:14). Thus Haggai's challenge to build the temple is grounded in the conviction that God is sovereign, that he takes the initiative in speaking to them through his prophet, that he has a purpose for them, that he makes demands on them, and that he will bless them.

Teaching about the temple

Haggai's main challenge to the returned exiles was that they should set aside their discouragement, their problems, and the work on their own land and houses that they felt must be completed before they could commit time and resources to building the temple. Haggai saw the temple as a focus for the life of the nation, a visible symbol that would raise their morale, reminding them and their opponents that God was with them. Completing it must be their first priority. Haggai was not reaffirming the superstitious reliance on the temple as a guarantee of prosperity which had characterized pre-exilic thinking.

The exile had shown that what mattered was relationship with God and heartfelt faith and obedience, not cultic ritual or temple worship on its own. But relationship with God must be expressed in some practical reality. Building the temple was a sign of their obedience and faith, and gave an opportunity for reasserting God's power and for God's glory, which had left the first temple (Ezekiel 10:1–22), to return. It was as if the work on the temple would enable God's activity and God's blessing to be unleashed. The temple would also be the focal point to which believers from all nations could come (2:7).

2:10–14 presents some difficulties. Haggai may be encouraging those who thought that working in the temple which had been so defiled by Babylonian troops would make them eternally unacceptable to God. However it is perhaps more likely that he is warning those who thought that working on God's temple in itself would make them especially holy.

Teaching about the Future

Haggai's vision for the restored community involved a new temple that was even more glorious than the first one (2:9), a life of prosperity in the land (2:19), God's rule being exercised through David's descendant, Zerubbabel

(2:23), and the 'shaking' of the whole of creation until God's purposes were carried out (2:6–8; 21–22). It is difficult to assess how far Haggai believed all this would take place immediately after the rebuilding of the temple and how far in a more distant future. The 'in a little while' of 2:6 implies a lapse of time, but there is also a strong sense of God working in the present.

If Haggai was speaking historically when he pictured Zerubbabel in messianic terms as God's signet-ring, and described the greater glory of the new temple, then he was mistaken. The Davidic monarchy was not restored and the temple was not as big as the old one. But if he was speaking eschatologically, emphasizing that David's line was not rejected for ever, and focusing on Zerubbabel as the contemporary symbol of the continuing Davidic coven-ant then that is a different matter. As for the temple, although its glory appeared less, yet Herod's temple, which was later seen as a development and extension of the second temple, could certainly be described as more glorious. Indeed, 2:2–3 may be suggesting that the glory of the old temple was largely external and God took his own glory away from there. This time God's spirit will be present (2:5), bringing a greater glory.

The ambiguity in the prophecy is perhaps deliberate, giving God the freedom to fulfil his own word in his own way. The messianic implications and the promises about the temple are more completely fulfilled in the coming of Christ at the incarnation, and carry our thoughts even beyond that to his coming at the end of time.

A TASTER IN HAGGAI

Haggai 2:23

'"On that day," declares the LORD Almighty,   23
    "I will take you, my servant Zerubbabel son of
    Shealtiel," declares the LORD, "and I will make

you like my signet ring, for I have chosen you,"
declares the LORD Almighty.'

'That day', is a standard formula referring to a time when
God will act decisively, changing the whole course of the
history of the universe. Haggai describes this as God
shaking the heavens and the earth (2:21). At that time,
Zerubbabel, the representative Davidic descendant, would
come into his proper role. The point of the comparison
with the signet ring is that Jehoiachin, the last acknowledged Davidic king had been described as a signet-ring
pulled off God's right hand (Jeremiah 22:24). Now Haggai
makes it clear that David's descendants are not rejected
for ever.

HAGGAI FOR TODAY

The letter to the Hebrews clearly implies that any call to
re-build the temple would not be appropriate for Christians
who through Christ have free access to the presence of
God. So is Haggai's prophecy now of historical interest
only? Not at all. Haggai reminds us that God does *sometimes* speak through economic circumstances. The challenge to listen to what God is saying and to get our
priorities right is a very powerful one. The returned exiles
had been given, and had accepted, a commission to
rebuild the temple. They had allowed on the one hand,
difficulties and discouragements, and on the other hand
concern for their own, perhaps legitimate, needs to prevent
them from fulfilling their commission. They had even got
to the stage of putting panelling (a great luxury) in their
own houses (1:4), while God's house was still neglected.

It is still easy to deceive ourselves in much the same
way. The concerns which prevent us from completing a
God-given task often appear legitimate and even essential.
As soon as we have paid off a reasonable proportion of
the mortgage, or got the garden looking the way we want
it, or seen the children through school, through university,

or married, *then* we will be able to think about what God wants. Haggai does not suggest that such concerns should be ignored, but he insists that obedience to God, (which may for some involve spending more time with the children and less with the church!) must come first. In this respect Haggai is a fore-runner of Jesus who said: 'Seek first his kingdom and his righteousness and all these things will be given to you as well' (Matthew 6:33).

CHAPTER 25

Zechariah

OUTLINE

THE PROPHET AND HIS BACKGROUND

Zechariah worked as a prophet at the same time as Haggai, but he seems to have been a different sort of person. Haggai had a straightforward, down to earth message, whereas Zechariah was a visionary. Chapters 1–8 of the book contain several of his visions, and also a number of his messages calling the people to action. It is worth noting that Zechariah, like Ezekiel (ch. 37), is a participant in the visions, not a mere observer. Chapters 9–14, which are undated, do not mention Zechariah at all. The dated prophecies are from between 520 and 518 BC and Zechariah shared Haggai's concern that the temple should be rebuilt and the community firmly established on a proper basis; that is, in dependence on and obedience to God.

The name Zechariah, meaning something like 'Yahweh Remembers', was common; about thirty different Zechariahs can be identified in the Old Testament. This one is described in 1:1, 7 as 'the son of Berekiah the son of Iddo'. In Ezra 5:1 and 6:14 he is referred to simply as the son of Iddo. This may be because Iddo was better known and the term 'son' is often used when 'grandson' is meant. However, Isaiah 8:2 mentions a Zechariah the son of Jerberekiah who was a reliable witness. It has been suggested that there has been confusion between these two and the name Berekiah was mistakenly added at some stage to the description in Zechariah. If, as seems likely but not absolutely certain, Nehemiah 12:4, 10, 16 refers to the same family, then Zechariah was a priest who eventually became head of the priestly clan of Iddo. In the Septuagint (the Greek version of the Old Testament), and other versions, a number of Psalms are associated with Zechariah including Psalms 111, 125, 137, and 145–150.

THE UNITY OF ZECHARIAH

As has already been hinted, there are several significant differences between chapters 1–8 and chapters 9–14 of Zechariah. It is not just that 9–14 have no dates and no reference to Zechariah, the whole background and outlook seems to be different. Chapters 1–8 are full of hope: although the situation has not been easy. Here, as in Haggai, we read of an immediate and positive response to the prophet's message. Chapters 9–14, say nothing about a rebuilding programme and refer only to disobedience and bad leadership. There is no mention of Darius, nor any other king, but in 9:13 Greece is referred to as the dominant power. Chapter 9 begins with a heading, which speaks of 'the burden of the word of Yahweh', a phrase not used in 1–8.

For these and other reasons most scholars agree that 9–14 should be assumed to come from a different source from the prophet Zechariah who was responsible for 1–8. A few would give 9–14 a date before the exile. Joseph Mede, a seventeenth century scholar, believed that Jeremiah wrote these chapters. He pointed out that in Matthew 27:9, words from Zechariah 11:12–13 are ascribed to Jeremiah. At the other extreme are those who place these chapters as late as the Maccabean times in the second century BC. However, a large majority of scholars conclude that the reference to Greece in 9:13 implies a date in the period of Greek power after Alexander the Great's invasion in 333 BC.

Just as there is debate over the date there is also disagreement as to whether or not these six chapters should be seen as a unity. Some identify two units, 9–11 and 12–14 and others suggest that these chapters contain a compilation of oracles from different sources. There is little evidence on these points and a search for an exact

date or for the precise structure of this section is somewhat
fruitless. However it would be wrong to ignore the fact
that as well as significant differences, there are also points
of similarity between the two sections of Zechariah. It is
not just that they are united by a sense of the ultimate
triumph of God and the eventual establishment of his
kingdom led by a chosen Messiah. In addition, both parts
make extensive use of earlier prophets, both stress the
need for repentance, the centrality of Jerusalem, and the
place of other nations. The Hebrew phrase translated by
'to and fro' in the RSV and 'come and go' and 'marauding'
in the NIV, occurs in Zechariah 7:14 and 9:8 but nowhere
else in the Old Testament, which seems to suggest some
connection between the two sections.

We should also note that Greece was becoming influential as early as the beginning of the fifth century BC. Isaiah
66:19, which is often dated at the same time as Zechariah
1–8, refers to Greece. It is just possible that if, as the
evidence from Ezra and Nehemiah suggests, the community in Judah regressed rather than progressed after
the completion of the temple in 515 BC, then Zechariah can
be seen as responsible for the whole book. This would
mean that 1–8 were written when Zechariah was a young
man and 9–14 many years later towards the end of his life.
Both the differences and the similarities could be accounted
for in this way. In any case the book has come to us as a
single unit and there is no evidence that either section
circulated independently. Whether 9–14 were there from
the beginning or introduced by an editor, the book displays
substantial unity, and we need to consider its impact as a
whole and not just as the sum of its two sections.

LITERARY FORM

An important question about the form of the book is
whether or not Zechariah should be seen as apocalyptic.
The term apocalyptic derives from the Greek word *apoka-
lypsis*, meaning 'revelation' or 'uncovering', as in Revelation

1:1. It is applied to a type of literature which was common in the years just before the coming of Christ and of which Revelation in the New Testament and Daniel in the Old Testament are the standard biblical examples. In general it is seen as differing from prophecy but it is recognized that the roots of biblical apocalyptic are to be found in the prophets and Zechariah is often cited as an example of this. This type of literature takes a known historical setting and develops it in a cosmic or supra-historical fashion, picturing the end of the present age as involving great battles between massive spiritual forces and a final decisive catastrophe before God intervenes in a cataclysmic fashion to bring in the new age. It is characterized by visions, often explained by an angelic interpreter, and by the use of imaginative imagery and fantastic symbolism.

Many characteristics of apocalyptic are absent from Zechariah and it cannot be seen as full-blown apocalyptic. However, certain aspects of the book may justify the description of Zechariah 1–8 as 'visionary apocalyptic' and of 9–14 with its descriptions of earthquakes and battles, God's intervention, and temporary defeat followed by ultimate victory, as 'prophetic apocalyptic'.

The book is systematically structured. In 1–8 the focus is the historical situation of 520–518 BC. The prophet insists that God will intervene in Judah's history to ensure that both the temple and the city of Jerusalem will be rebuilt, that the nations will be scattered and defeated and that God's people will be cleansed from sin. Zechariah envisaged that the high priest, Joshua, and the governor, Zerubbabel, would unite in serving Yahweh and fulfilling his purposes. P. Lamarche argues that 9–14 shows an orderly progress, moving from the judgment and salvation of neighbouring peoples (9:1–8) through a repeated stress on war and the victory of Israel (9:11–10:1; 10:3b–11:3; 12:1–9; 14:1–15), to judgment and salvation for all nations (14:16–19). Details of Lamarche's analysis can be found in Joyce Baldwin: *Haggai, Zechariah, Malachi* IVP 1972 p. 77–79.

The book thus moves from consideration of events in the history of Israel and the relationship there between good and evil, to describing the conflict between good and evil in the world as a whole and finally the events at the end of time. Uniting these different sections is a common emphasis on 'the need for repentance, the certainty of judgment, the continuing mercy of God and the Messianic figure who accomplishes his purposes.' (Baldwin p. 81).

THE MESSAGE OF ZECHARIAH

Zechariah has often been seen as not only the longest of the twelve so called 'minor' prophets, but as the most obscure, and most difficult to understand. But the book plays a significant role in the New Testament. It is quoted regularly in the passion narratives, Zechariah 9–14 being referred to even more times than Isaiah 40–55, and it also had a major influence on the book of Revelation. It deserves to be taken seriously. If the prophecies of Haggai, Amos, or even Jeremiah can be described as blueprints setting out God's plans and purposes for the future, then we would have to see Zechariah as more like an abstract painting. The canvas as a whole is meaningful, but whereas in some places the detailed meaning is obvious, in some it must be gleaned from the impression given by colour and texture, while in other places some knowledge of the symbolism used by the painter is essential for complete understanding.

The main aim of chapters 1–8 is apparently to describe God working out his purposes and to challenge the people to play their part in achieving these goals. The challenge is set out clearly in 1:3–5, and expanded in 6:9 – 7:13. It can be summarized as 'Repent, turn away from your evil ways and your evil practices and live your lives as God intended, care for the needy and "administer true justice, show mercy and compassion to one another"' (1:4; 7:9). God's purposes and the action that God will take are set out pictorially in the visions and clarified in chapter 8.

It is noteworthy that the angelic guide gives only a very

basic interpretation of the visions. We should beware of attempting to supply a precise meaning for every detail; they function as impressions rather than intricate allegories. On the one hand, there is total certainty that God will act and that his purposes will be worked out. On the other hand there is a clear recognition that this will not happen in a comfortable, peaceful or easy way. On the contrary, there will be great battles, both within the nation and in a worldwide or even cosmic setting, before God's perfect new age can come. Zechariah stresses that the strength of the evil opponent must not be underestimated; at times he may indeed appear to be successful. But in spite of this, God the King will ultimately triumph.

Throughout the prophecy God's grace is emphasized. The good news that Zechariah proclaimed to the people was that God in his grace would restore and renew them, bringing them both personal forgiveness and cleansing and also material blessing and prosperity. This work of grace would be centred on Zion. Like Haggai, Zechariah saw the rebuilding of God's temple as the catalyst which would enable God's work to commence. The people were challenged to live lives worthy of all that God would do for them.

Zerubbabel and Joshua are important figures in Zechariah, as they are in Haggai. However, Zechariah does not seem to attach messianic significance to Zerubbabel. Although the book speaks often of the messianic messenger, it generally does so in an eschatological context, referring to God's action in the end times, rather than in the immediate historical situation. God's messenger is described as taking away sin, and as establishing a new rule of peace (3:4,10; 9:9–10), as the Branch (6:12), the priestly ruler and mighty king (6:13; 9:9–10; 14:9,16). He will come in humility and also in glory (9:9; 14:4), will be betrayed for thirty pieces of silver (11:12–13), struck by God's sword and yet be so close to God that their purposes will be identical (13:7). From the very beginning of the Christian era Zechariah was seen as an important source for messianic prophecy and Matthew 21:5; 27:9, Mark 14:27, Luke 21:24

and John 19:37 are just some of the gospel verses which refer to Zechariah and apply his prophecy to Jesus.

Zechariah's portrayal of the future is in general positive, but includes a recognition that final victory will come only in the face of fierce opposition. Jerusalem itself will be all but defeated (12:1–3; 14:1–2), but God himself will protect the community, acting as their shepherd when human shepherds fail and fighting on their behalf (9:14–10:12; 14:3–4). The nations will be judged (12:9; 14:12–15) in a stupendous episode involving nature itself (14:4–10). Eventually even the nations will join in pilgrimage to worship of Yahweh the King and Jerusalem will become in reality a holy city (14:16–21).

TASTERS IN ZECHARIAH

Zechariah 5:1–4

I looked again—and there before me was a
   flying scroll!
He asked me, 'What do you see?'   2
I answered, 'I see a flying scroll, thirty feet long
   and fifteen feet wide.'
And he said to me, 'This is the curse that is going   3
   out over the whole land; for according to what it
   says on one side, every thief will be banished, and
   according to what it says on the other, everyone who
   swears falsely will be banished.
The LORD Almighty declares, "I will send it out,   4
   and it will enter the house of the thief and the
   house of him who swears falsely by my name. It
   will remain in his house and destroy it, both its
   timbers and its stones." '

One of the simplest of Zechariah's eight visions is this picture of a flying scroll. The description follows the same pattern as the second and third visions (1:18–2:13). The scroll that Zechariah saw was gigantic. The measurements are the same as those of the porch at the front of Solomon's temple (1 Kings 6:3) and possibly the same as the tabernacle. However, it is not obvious that there is any significance in this fact. The scroll's size, and the fact that it was open and flying and not rolled up in a cupboard, signify that it is there to be read by everyone. It is said to represent God's curse. Deuteronomy 27:9–26 and 28:15–68 enumerate some of the disasters that will befall those who break God's covenant, and it is apparently this covenant curse that is meant here. Before there could be a new start, and a cleansing of land, temple and people, the curse must function. The sins mentioned are robbery, and treating God's name lightly; symbolic of all sins against other people and sins against God. Such behaviour can have no place in God's kingdom and Zechariah thus emphasizes that wrongdoing is no trivial matter.

Zechariah 10:3–5

'My anger burns against the shepherds,   3
  and I will punish the leaders;
  for the LORD Almighty will care for his flock,
  the house of Judah,
  and make them like a proud horse in battle.
From Judah will come the cornerstone,   4
  from him the tent-peg,
  from him the battle-bow,
  from him every ruler.
Together they will be like mighty men   5
  trampling the muddy streets in battle.
Because the LORD is with them,
  they will fight and overthrow the horsemen.

These verses bring together a number of the themes of Zechariah and illustrate his use of traditional prophetic ideas, bringing together the imagery of the shepherd and the flock and the warrior in battle. In verse 2 Zechariah has expressed his concern for the present state of the community, an oppressed and leaderless flock, deceived by false religion. Now he looks to the future; condemning the present, so-called, leaders he offers reassurance that God himself will take action on behalf of his own people. The disorganized sheep will be transformed into a war-horse, trained and ready for battle. Because God will be with them they will be champions in battle, defeating their enemies. The 'cornerstone', 'tent-peg', 'battle-bow' and 'every ruler', in verse 4 emphasize security and stability on the one hand and action and power on the other.

ZECHARIAH FOR TODAY

As we have already seen, the way the New Testament uses Zechariah helps us to benefit from the light the book throws on the role of Jesus as messiah. The New Testament use also brings out Zechariah's keen awareness of God's final action in history, and helps us to understand the implications of this. Equally significant is the manner in which Zechariah utilizes and re-interprets earlier material, deriving contemporary relevance from messages given to previous generations. His book stands as a proto-type for the interpretation of prophecy.

For many people Zechariah's teaching, in its own right, has been a source of great encouragement. It carries the assurance that God will act as shepherd when human shepherds fail, and affirms the certainty of ultimate victory and triumph. In addition, however, it recognizes that this ultimate victory is achieved only after great difficulties and times of apparent defeat. Thus Zechariah offers help in restoring confidence to those who face apparently hopeless situations and who can scarcely see beyond the fierceness of the present battle. Zechariah never underestimates the strength of the enemy, whether Judah's local opponents or the spiritual forces opposing God's work. He challenges his hearers to take seriously the attacks of Satan in today's world and in their own lives.

But Zechariah points beyond such opposition to the

power of God who stands with his people in the fight, and with whose help they can defeat evil. The prophet brought good news to his contemporaries, prophesying that God would send his messiah to help and save them. In Jesus Christ we can see many of those prophecies fulfilled. But Zechariah looks beyond the first coming of the messiah to the end of history when the same messiah will finally and fully triumph over evil. Like the community in the sixth century, the people of God today are to show concern for justice, righteousness and the care of the needy, and to wait with excitement and with confidence for God's intervention in the future and the coming of his kingdom.

CHAPTER 26

Malachi

UNITY AND AUTHORSHIP

The book of Malachi records the work of the last known prophet in the pre-Christian era and also forms a fitting end to the Old Testament. There is very little distinctive or new in Malachi but he offers a good summary of prophetic teaching, and the reference in the concluding verses to the law of Moses and Elijah is perhaps an intentional bringing together of the whole of the Old Testament. The message of Malachi is straightforward and easy to understand, uncomplicated by the symbolism and imagery present in Zechariah. But the impact of Malachi should not be underestimated, it is hard-hitting and uncompromising: failing a response to the message, then there is no more to be said. However, Malachi also shows a profound pastoral concern. He was anxious that both those who have responded to God and those who have not should know the meaning of the love of God and grasp what being in a covenant relationship with him entails.

We know virtually nothing of the prophet himself, not even his name, many would say. Malachi, meaning 'my messenger', is not known as a name elsewhere in the Old Testament; the word is translated in the Greek version, the Septuagint, as a description rather than a name, and the same expression is found in 3:1. The fact that the

introductory verse is very similar to both Zechariah 9:1
and 12:1 has led some to suggest that the Old Testament
ends with three anonymous prophecies. However, the
book as we have it does form a unity, it would be very
unusual for such a prophecy to be anonymous, and the
introduction would be very clumsy, involving both a third
person and a first person expression in the same sentence.
One later tradition identifies Malachi with Ezra, but there
is no real justification for this. Whether 'Malachi' is a title
or a name, it is appropriate that a prophet who concen-
trates so much on the direct words of God to Judah should
be described as God's messenger.

There is very little debate about the unity of the book of
Malachi. It has been suggested that the negative attitude
to foreign nations seen in 2:11 contradicts the more positive
approach in 1:11, but the only verses that are seriously
questioned are 4:4–6 which are said to be unrelated to the
previous verses and therefore to have been added as a
conclusion to the whole Old Testament. This may be so,
but the verses fit well with the message of Malachi as a
whole, suitably ending his message with a focus on the
covenant.

BACKGROUND AND DATE

There are no detailed historical references which might
enable us to date the prophecy accurately, but we can be
fairly certain that it comes from about the same time as
Ezra and Nehemiah. The word used in 1:8 to refer to the
governor, found also in Haggai 1:1 and Nehemiah 5:14, is
used only in a post-exilic context. The temple is fully
operational and enough time has elapsed since its completion in 515 BC for the worship to have became corrupted.
The conditions are very similar to those described in Ezra
and Nehemiah: there are problems of intermarriage and
business partnerships with non-Judeans; the poor are
oppressed; there is no real sense of community identity or
brotherhood, and general indifference to God and his

demands. Nehemiah 13 in particular provides a helpful background to Malachi.

The oracles cannot have been delivered during the period when Nehemiah himself was governor, because he did not accept the contributions from the people described in 1:8 (Nehemiah 5:14). Nehemiah was governor from 445–434 BC after which he returned to Susa for some time before taking up the governorship for a further period. We cannot really be sure whether Malachi prophesied before Nehemiah came on the scene, or in the time when Nehemiah was back in Susa. Perhaps the fact that Malachi shows no awareness of any reforms supports the earlier date. In either case, about a hundred years have passed since the return from exile and to all intents and purposes the community seems to be in exactly the same state of compromise and failure to keep the covenant that the pre-exilic prophets had complained about. Judah had not learned the lessons that the exile should have taught them.

STYLE AND STRUCTURE

These oracles almost certainly originated as speeches rather than as written documents. With the possible exception of 4:4–6 there is very little sign of editorial activity; they seem to have been written up almost exactly as first preached. We have no way of knowing if the prophet himself wrote down the speeches or if they were recorded by somebody else. As a point of interest we may note that in the Hebrew there are only three chapters, with 4:1–6 in the English versions appearing as 3:19–24. (Chapter divisions are in any case always somewhat arbitrary, as none of the original material was delivered in that form.)

The prophecies take the form of a dialogue between God and the people; or more accurately, statements are made by God, after which he introduces rhetorical questions supposedly raised by the people and then gives

answer to these questions. The prophet is clearly determined that the Judeans will realize that his message is
what God himself is saying to them. Forty-seven of the
book's fifty-five verses contain direct speech from God.
The phrase 'says the LORD almighty' (or 'Yahweh of
hosts') occurs 21 times, 'says the LORD' twice and once,
at the centre of the book in 2:16, we have, 'says the LORD
God of Israel'. This debate, or dialogue style is occasionally
found elsewhere, for example in Jeremiah 13:12–14, 22:8–9,
Ezekiel 11:2–4, 18:1–32 and Amos 5:16–27. However, only
in Malachi is it used so consistently.

OUTLINE

THE MESSAGE OF MALACHI

There is a strange tension in the book of Malachi. De-
pending on one's starting point, the message can come
across either as fiercely condemnatory and somewhat
legalistic, or else as a gentle reminder of God's love and
an encouragement for his people. This tension is, at least
to some extent, resolved when we notice how much of
Malachi's attention is focused on the covenant. The book

is full of the words of the covenant God, 'Yahweh the God
of Israel' (2:16). In a way that is very reminiscent of
Deuteronomy, it speaks of what this covenant God is like,
and what is expected of those who are in covenant
relationship with him. It describes the great blessings that
will come to those who keep the covenant and the curses
awaiting those who are unfaithful to it and break their
promises. The stark terms in which Malachi describes
their behaviour leaves no doubt that he expects most of
them, unless they change their behaviour, to receive the
curses rather than the blessings. It was because they had
forgotten or doubted the reality of divine judgment that
they were asking questions about the lack of evidence of
God's love and his apparent failure to fulfil his promises.
It is possible that Malachi is expounding the implications
of the covenant renewal that had been introduced by Ezra.
Alternatively, and perhaps more likely he may be providing
the background teaching on covenant that made it easier
for Ezra's teaching to be understood and accepted.

The God of the Covenant

Malachi is in no sense intended to be a doctrinal treatise
on the nature of God, but, not least because so much of
the book records God's own words, it is shot through with
a sense of God's reality. He is Yahweh Almighty, the great
king who deserves respect and honour (1:6, 14). He sits
in judgment and his decisions will be absolutely just.
Doing justice involves punishing the guilty, but the righteous need not fear. God knows all about them and they
can feel utterly secure (2:17; 3:3–6; 3:16; 4:2). His relationship with Judah is like that of a father with his son (1:6;
3:17). He loves them and wants to provide for them and
bless them (3:10–12) but he also seeks their love in return.
God is active, personal and involved; he loves and he
hates (1:2–3; 2:11, 16), he can be angered or wearied (1:4;
2:17), and pleased or displeased (1:10, 13; 3:4).

A major aim of the book seems to be to reassure the

people of God's love for them. The temple has been rebuilt, but there seems to be very little sign of any returning glory. Is God powerless, or does he not care for them? On the contrary, says Malachi, he still loves them and longs to enjoy a covenant relationship with them. God is not changeable (3:6), his promises stand firm and will be fulfilled, but these promises, like the covenant itself, have always been conditional. God has not failed in his covenant obligations; he has done everything possible to encourage and enable them to fulfil theirs; but their responsibility cannot be ignored.

God's Expectations from Judah

The covenant obligations are taken for granted in Malachi rather than expounded in detail but their outline is clear. God expects from his people honour, love and obedience. Their worship must be wholehearted, sincere, and in accordance with the requirements of the law (1:6–14; 3:6–12). Similarly, he expects them to behave towards one another with justice and generosity (3:5). 2:5–7 contains a remarkable summary of what is expected of the priests. They should revere God and stand in awe of his name, give true instruction, live righteously and lead others to do the same. 'For the lips of a priest ought to preserve knowledge, and from his mouth men should seek instruction — because he is the messenger of the Lord Almighty'. In 2:10–16, we have another striking miniature, this time of the covenant ideal for marriage: man and wife united by a common faith and mutual loyalty, living together in loving partnership and bringing up their children to be godly. Malachi's condemnation of divorce is as strong as any found in the Old or the New Testaments.

Judah's Behaviour

The life of the community fell far short of these expectations. Part of this was failure in cultic worship. Not only was their worship hypocritical, but the offerings presented were second-rate and unacceptable (1:7–14). Far from teaching the people how to keep the covenant, the priests were actually leading them into violating it. There was failure too in the area of social responsibility. The legal system was unjust (2:9) and society was littered with broken marriages, immorality and oppression (2:14; 3:5).

But perhaps worse than this setting aside of both the ritual and the moral law was their behaviour towards God. Their religion was marginal to their lives. They acted not so much as if God did not exist, but as if he were of no account. They patronized him, treating him as if he could be manipulated and pacified with the minimum of effort. Far from showing God the honour he deserved, or being in awe of his great glory, they treated him with contempt. They could and should have been 'a righteous nation, a pure and devoted priesthood, happy homes, God-fearing children, and a people characterized by truth, integrity, generosity, gratitude, fidelity and love'. In fact they were characterized by 'smugness, pride and compromise' (R. L. Alden *Expositor's Bible Commentary Vol 7* p. 704, Zondervan 1985, edited by F. E. Gaebelein). It was their failure to live as God intended and not any failure in God's promises that was responsible for the lack of prosperity in the land and the absence of divine glory from the temple.

The Covenant Blessings and Curses

Malachi is clear and uncompromising about the future. Just as the obligations of the covenant were clearly laid out in the law, so were the consequences of both keeping it and breaking it. Like the Israelites of the time of Amos, the people seem to have assumed that if God was able to act, then any intervention by him in history would automatically be for their benefit. Like Amos, Malachi showed his contemporaries how wrong this perception was. God would most certainly act at a time that had already been appointed. But when the Lord came it would be in judgment to refine and test them. Those who failed that test would bring upon themselves the covenant curses which would undoubtedly destroy them. (2:2–3, 9; 3:1–4; 4:1).

But for the righteous who passed, like pure gold, through the refiner's fire, the story would be very different. In spite of these warnings Malachi was not disheartened. He fully expected some would respond to God's word (3:16–18). As God's treasured possession they would be spared from the consequences of the curses that would destroy the rest (3:17–18). Their names already known to God, they would ultimately join in worship which he would gladly accept (1:11; 3:3–4). Malachi was not really concerned with the position of other nations although he affirmed God's sovereignty over them (1:5). But people from all nations would eventually join in the continuous worship of Israel's great God (1:11).

The idea of a fore-runner, one who will come before the Messiah and prepare the way for him, referred to as 'the prophet Elijah' (4:5) is found only in Malachi. It has been suggested that Malachi identified himself as 'my messenger' in 3:1, and thus that he expected the day of Yahweh and the coming of the Messiah to be almost immediate. But there is no clear indication that this is so.

A TASTER IN MALACHI

Malachi 3:10–12

'Bring the whole tithe into the storehouse, that   10
   there may be food in my house. Test me in this,'
   says the LORD Almighty, 'and see if I will not
   throw open the floodgates of heaven and pour out
   so much blessing that you will not have room
   enough for it.
'I will prevent pests from devouring your crops,   11

and the vines in your fields will not cast their fruit,'
says the LORD Almighty.
'Then all the nations will call you blessed, for yours   12
will be a delightful land,' says the LORD Almighty.

These verses, perhaps the best known in Malachi, must be
seen in the context of the dialogue which precedes them.
In verses 7–9, the people are accused of turning away from
God and commanded to return to him. On asking what
actions are required of them, they are told to cease robbing
God by not bringing the tithes and offerings that are his
due. By robbing God in this way they have put themselves
under the curses of the covenant, but verses 10–12 offer
an alternative way forward, demonstrating the positive
side of the covenant. Malachi challenges them to put God
to the test by showing the total commitment God requires.
If they play their part then God will respond. Let them
indicate their commitment by bringing their full tithes,
then he will pour out blessing on them. The terminology
may be metaphorical or it may be that the opening of the
'floodgates of heaven' refers to the rain that would drive
the devouring locusts away, enabling the crops to grow
and thus bringing prosperity. In either case, the result will
be a 'delightful land' to live in and all nations will
recognize that God is on their side.

Malachi's words should be understood as a one-off
invitation to these particular people and not as a universal
precept that all who tithe will automatically receive rich
material blessings. The only general principle involved is
that if God's people will play their part, then God will
respond to their self-giving.

MALACHI FOR TODAY

Malachi spoke to a situation where the most common
attitude to religion was disillusioned boredom, and where
God was mocked or ignored more often than feared and
honoured: a situation not unlike that in many parts of the

world today. Malachi's clear, straightforward message setting out the reality of God, of the choices facing the people and of the action that God would take as a result of their choices has considerable relevance today.

We can still use philosophical questions as a means to blame God and to divert attention from our own short-comings. But the existence of such questions does not change God, nor the force of either his love or his judgment. Hard times no more indicate God's lack of love in today's world than in the time of Malachi. And now, as then, there is ample evidence of that love, if we will only look for it. The challenge to faithful leadership, faithful marriage and faithful living remains as sharp for the new covenant as for the old. As Verhoef says, 'Malachi's remarkable ethical thrust has lost none of its cutting edge. His teaching, both positive and negative, strikes at the heart of nominal, easy-going Christianity just as it did that of Judaism.' (p. 184 *Haggai and Malachi* Eerdmans 1987). Treating God with contempt is just as common today as then, and equally dangerous. Honouring God and living to please him is equally demanding today and just as rewarding.

Malachi with its summary of the Mosaic covenant and its urgent challenge to God's covenant people, provides a fitting close to the Old Testament and a fitting point of departure into the New.

SECTION IV: FURTHER STUDY

QUESTIONS FOR STUDY AND DISCUSSION

1. Summarize the message of Ezekiel and analyse the difficulties he faced in communicating this message.

2. Consider the influence of Ezekiel's visions on the rest of his ministry.

3. Compare and contrast the life and work of Jeremiah and Ezekiel.

4. Examine Ezekiel's teaching on the nature of responsibility.

5. Ezekiel's message of hope and deliverance could not be given until the exiled people had fully grasped the extent and the consequences of their sin. Are there elements of the Christian message which require previous knowledge or experience in order to be properly understood?

6. What kind of 'stumbling blocks' (Ezekiel 14:3) could prevent Christians today from hearing God's word?

7. With Ezekiel's concept of leadership in mind, assess your own attitudes and behaviour in any situation where you might be seen as 'in charge'.

8. In general, the prophets seem to emphasize the importance of attitudes and behaviour. Why do you think Haggai saw something external like the building of the temple as so significant?

9. Assess the effectiveness of Haggai's ministry.

10. Are there any apparently legitimate concerns which could prevent Christians or churches today from fulfilling the priorities which God may have for them?

11. What teaching about the Messiah is found in Zechariah?.

12. Examine the attitude of Zechariah and Haggai towards Zerubbabel.

13. In what ways can Zechariah be a challenge and an encouragement to Christians today?

14. Zechariah was very conscious of the spiritual forces at work in the world and the spiritual battles facing God's people. Think about the spiritual battles faced by the church today.

15. Explain Malachi's understanding of the covenant obligations.

16. Discuss the appropriateness of Malachi's response to the disillusionment and apathy of his fellow-countrymen.

17. Malachi insists that the covenant curses will be followed through by God just as much as the covenant blessings. Does this have any relevance today?

18. Is there any way in which you, or your church, could be accused of 'robbing God'? If so, how could this state of affairs best be reversed?

19. Do you think Malachi is an appropriate finale to the Old Testament canon? Give reasons for your answer.

SUGGESTED FURTHER READING

Eichrodt, W. *Ezekiel* (Old Testament Library) SCM 1970
Taylor, J. B. *Ezekiel* (Tyndale OTC) IVP 1969
Wevers, J. W. *Ezekiel* (New Century Bible) Oliphants 1969
Zimmerli, W. *Ezekiel* 2 vols. (Hermeneia) Fortress 1979, 1983
Baldwin, J. *Haggai, Zechariah, Malachi* (Tyndale OTC) IVP 1972
Coggins, R. J. *Haggai, Zechariah, Malachi* (Old Testament Guides) JSOT 1987
Kaiser, W. C. *Malachi* Baker 1984
Meyers, C. L. and E. M. Meyers *Haggai, Zechariah 1–8* (Anchor Bible) Doubleday 1987
Verhoef, P. A. *Haggai and Malachi* (NICOT) Eerdmans 1987
Smith, R. L. *Micah – Malachi* Word Biblical Commentaries 1984

INDEX OF MAJOR SUBJECTS

Some of the references noted here are very brief, some are of major significance, but the index as a whole should help you to trace the way in which various themes and ideas come across in different prophetic books.